WHAT NO ONE IS TELLING YOU ABOUT ADDICTIONS

HELEN GLOWACKI

Forward by Daniel Patrick Landolfi

Interior Photography by Matthew Burniston
Photo edit and overlay by Colette van Loggerenberg

Novels by Helen Gumienny Glowacki

When God Broke Grandma's Heart
When God Took Grandma Home
When Grandma Chased the Spirits
The Granddaughter and the Monkey Swing
The Story of God's Plan of Salvation
Abiding Faith, Hidden Treasure
And Then They Asked God

Non-Fiction Books by Helen Glowacki

Politically Incorrect: A Get Some Gumption Handbook When Enough is Enough!
What No One Is Telling You about Addictions
Overcoming Depression: How To Be Happy

The Why God Why Series by Helen Glowacki

To What Purpose?
Why God Why?
Why Trust Scripture?
What Should I Know About Life after Death And The Coming Tribulation?
Do Our Little Sins Really Count?
What Does God Want Me To Do RIGHT NOW?

****

Authors Website: www.Helenglowacki.com

Face book: http://www.facebook.com/pages/The-Grandmother-Series/155300907853909?ref=ts

WHAT NO ONE IS TELLING YOU ABOUT ADDICTIONS

HELEN GLOWACKI

Forward by Daniel Patrick Landolfi

Interior Photography by Matthew Burniston
Photo edit and overlay by Colette van Loggerenberg

Library of Congress Control Number:
ISBN Hardcover
Softcover ISBN 978-1-4507-9075-8
EBook ISBN

This book was printed in the United States of America

The King James Version (KJV) of the Bible, which is public domain in the United States of America, is used for all scriptural references throughout this book. The information contained herein is based upon the opinion, research and religious belief of the author. Matters pertaining to one's spiritual life, or application of the information contained herein should be discussed with a theological professional.

Interior photography by Matthew Burniston, UK
Photo edit and overlay by Colette van Loggerenberg, SA

To order additional copies of this book visit:
www.Helenglowacki.com
For more information email the author at:
helen@helenglowacki.com

MISSION STATEMENT

TO SERVE GOD

WITH ALL

OUR STRENGTH

AND ALL

OUR HEART

Helen Gumienny Glowacki, Daniel Patrick Landolfi

Photography by Matthew Burniston
Verse overlay by Colette van Loggerenberg

FORWARD

by Daniel Patrick Landolfi

To Those Who Suffer From Addiction:

The realities of addiction are simple - we let our bodies run our lives. We allow our flesh to take control and demand from us whatever it wants. Our flesh wants what it wants, when it wants it, and thus seeks complete control. Our emotions play a large part in how we react to the demands of the flesh and therefore how we develop addictions. What we feel triggers or activates an auto-response which causes us to act in a way which brings relief and appears to fulfill our desires.

Because we have responded in certain ways in the past which appeared to fulfill our needs, we seek to activate them again. But as we do the same thing over and over again, two things begin to occur: it becomes easier to do and it becomes harder and harder to stop. As an example, if we had a rough day at work, we often raid the refrigerator to bring fleshly relief as soon as we arrive home. But whenever those feelings resurface, our flesh wants to resort to whatever seemed to work in the past to bring relief. Another example is the person who has a rough day and develops the tendency to have a drink to find relief… and in time they find themselves in a position where they *must* have that drink and many more. This need can be stirred by a number of situations even one as simple as having to make a difficult decision. In time, an addiction to alcohol can develop.

Many things influence us in this world and this is why it is important for us to learn the proper way to handle our feelings. Those things which influence us are hardships, confusion, depression, thoughts of suicide, loss, fear, anxiety and many other emotions and situations. If we don't learn how to recognize and attend our feelings, Satan will use them to allow his spirits to engage us and tempt us again, and soon we become enslaved.

Addiction is a cry of the flesh yearning for something it is used to getting or feels it needs and wants. It's the body wanting the control to tell you that it wants something so badly it is willing to react until you yield and give it what it wants. It can be very difficult to live day to day going through these temptations. But this is why Jesus told us also to meditate upon His Words day and night (Joshua 1:8) and to keep our minds refreshed and renewed (Romans 12:2). Loving God means that we begin by learning what God wants us to know because as it says in Philippians 2:15, "That ye may prove yourselves".

Our struggle is to become someone who is not led by their flesh, but by Christ who teaches us that we are a three part being: spirit, soul, and body (1 Thess. 5:23) and that if we live by placing those three in that order we will be successful while if we live according first to body, then soul and lastly by sprit we will fail and become subject to Satan

Do you feel that pull of the body? Do you feel your body demanding satisfaction? Are you drawn to enter every time you pass a liquor store, thinking about the liquid sparkling in the cup, swirling around in the glass, begging you, pleading with you to just take one sip; to just have one drink? Do you believe that you can just smoke one joint or use hard drugs only when you choose to do so and not when the spirit which controls your body demands it?

This is because we have been conditioned to be led by our feelings. It is because of the way we think when we tell ourselves: "I feel like…", "I want to …", "I have to….", "I'll only…." These are all signs that we are led by our emotions and this is where our emotions become dangerous. As long as we are being led by our emotions we are not being led by the spirit of God. Does this happen to you? Do you feel desperate if your body doesn't get its daily dose of alcohol…or drugs….or pornography…or any other fleshly desire?

Even David understood the pull these addictions can have on us. In Proverbs 23:31 David said, "Don't gaze at the wine, seeing how red it is, how it sparkles in the cup, how smoothly it goes down." Yet isn't this what we do? We entertain thoughts about how it looks, tastes, and feels. We think about the satisfaction we feel while we indulge. We want it, we can feel it, and we believe that we deserve it, need it. We allow ourselves to get so built up about what we want that we can no longer resist it. And then we do it. Again...., perhaps thinking that next time, we won't. Whatever it is, we partake of it, and after the deed is done, all we can think about is how we feel at the moment and either when the next fix is coming or how weak and unworthy we are.

As we grow older, we learn that there are certain spirits which have influence over us. Some we hardly notice but they cause us to feel rejection, fear, depression, insecurity or pride- things which weigh us down and play havoc with our emotions. These spirits pull on our bodies and send us into the arms of even stronger spirits which cause us to turn to fleshly relief instead of looking to the word of God. These spirits and our reactions to them prohibit us from moving forward in Christ.

But there is hope. There is life. And it's waiting for you. There are people praying for you, even if you don't know it or believe it. God does have a special plan for you. God knew you were going to go through this. He knew you were going to have this stumbling block. And He knew it was going to be a hard journey. He loves you. I love you. Many people love you. It might not "feel" that way. It might not "look" that way. You see, God knows all things; He knows your past, present, and future. He has called you to be a witness for Him. He still has a special purpose and plan for you. But you have to make that first step. You have to get it ingrained into your spirit that you want to change and believe that His plans and goals outweigh the temporary satisfaction which you seek.

My prayer is that as you read this book you begin to understand that first, you are not alone. Many of us, in secret and in the open, deal with our own addictions, some minor, some not so minor. A lot of us have hit bottom and have felt the sin and sadness weigh heavily upon our hearts. But before healing can take place, change needs to be sought.
I know this, because God also has a plan for me too. Just as I am writing this forward to help you, and this book is written to teach you, God ordained both through imperfect people to share with you His love. He will use you for the same great cause. He believes in you and so do I.

Daniel Landolfi

(Daniel Landolfi has been a youth counselor for over ten years as well as a student of psychology for seven. Working with people, he has seen how a small seed of courage can blossom into an enormous tree. Daniel also sits on the board of a local charity, Rebuilding Families Foundation, and Children of Tomorrow Foundation, Intl')

ACKNOWLEDGEMENTS

Special thanks to Daniel Patrick Landolfi who wrote the forward for this book and who assists me in many different areas of my work. To Colette van Loggerenberg of Pietermaritzburg, South Africa, who provides or edits the photography and verse overlays used in this series, helps promote my books in South Africa, and distributes many to cancer centers, drug rehabilitation centers, prisons and other areas where there may be souls who hunger to learn of God.

My thanks to Matthew Burniston for the photography he provided for this book which he captured in the UK. To Michele Mascatello, Great Falls, Virginia, Andre E. Myrick of Washington, DC, Daniel Byers of St. Petersburg, Florida and Mwanda Bermudes from Lusaka, Zambia for the exquisite photographs used in some of the other books in this series.

Very special love goes to my husband Wally, the love of my life who does so much to support me and to make my computer behave; and to my very special children and grandchildren for their loving and constant encouragement.

Thanks to Rev. Kevin Speranza for locating and developing additional venues for the distribution of my books and for his comments, courage and support. To my brothers and sisters and ministers in faith who have provided their prayers and love, and to my Face book friends who pray for me and also support this ministry.

And I would be remiss if I did not mention the loving support of Kathy Leipp from Germany, and Raphael Wyngaart and Ambrose Damon from South Africa.

Special thanks also to District Apostle Charles Ndandula, Zambia, Africa; to District Apostle (Ret.) Richard Freund, Virginia, USA; Apostle Reinhard

Hecht, North Carolina, USA; and Priest Herold Ambrose, Palm Beach Gardens, Florida, USA for their incredible support and powerful prayers.

But most of all, we thank our Heavenly Father for His inspiration, guiding hand, protection, and never-ending love. May this work bring joy to His heart and help find that last soul!

Photography by Colette van Loggerenberg

Thus saith the Lord of hosts: It shall come to pass that there shall come people and the inhabitants of many cities....saying, Let us go speedily to pray before the Lord and to seek the Lord of hosts: I will go also."

Zechariah 8:20-21

MESSAGE FROM THE AUTHOR

Few people are willing to talk about their addictions and fewer discuss their failure to overcome them. Blaringly absent from most conversations is what scripture tells us about addictions and what, or more correctly said, *who,* causes those addictions.

Throughout scripture God protects us by describing what we must guard against and how we are to care for our physical, emotional and spiritual well-being. While many believe that scripture only addresses our questions about how to prepare for and obtain our soul salvation, and develop an intimate relationship with God, scripture also provides guidelines to keep us safe.

Not only has God provided information about what we should do to prepare for life after death, and for the imminent time of tribulation, but tells us how to prepare for and rebuff attacks from Satan which are launched against us to prevent us from obtaining our soul salvation. Scripture warns us that evil is alive and well and on the attack and also tells us why. Further, it explains how many of these attacks can affect our health and well being.

Most of us acknowledge that our life on earth will determine our position in Heaven, yet few understand that God has clearly said that many will lose their faith before Christ returns. Through scripture we learn that despite God's warnings, many will be unable to retain their faith, will blame God for their suffering and for not intervening, and will lose their soul salvation because of this. Their lack of understanding about what Satan does and why and what power he will have during the end times will cause them to falter.

Thus, learning what scripture tells us and what is required to prepare for the return of Christ is imperative. So also is learning how to avoid the traps that Satan will lay for us. God does not look only upon our failures but He looks into our hearts and can see all things…especially those things which we try to hide from others…. sometimes even from our selves.

Spiritually, scripture expresses God's desire to forgive us for our failures, explains what is required to become the Bride of Christ, or a King, or Priest, or a Saint in the kingdom of heaven, and warns us why many, when judged, will be thrown into the Lake of Fire with Satan for all eternity.

Scripture also teaches us that we have a powerful enemy who wants us to lose our faith, not be completed in the eyes of God, and uses those who do not know God's words, or who sin with little or no remorse, to bring harm to the children of God. Scripture was, and is the word of God. It is perfect and it is complete. What we learn from scripture can bring us into fellowship with our Heavenly Father, and into the completion which is necessary to become the Bride for Christ.

But scripture also brings us dire warnings about what Satan does, what his powers are and how the fallen angels who left heaven with Satan can invade the soul of mankind. Sadly, few understand this concept and are caught in the subtle traps with which Satan can bring us under his power and captivity and thereby prevent us from becoming the Bride of Christ.

The goal of this book and all the books in this series is to answer in an easy-to-understand manner the many questions we have about scripture and what God offers which will help us overcome what Satan brings us. It is to explain what is required to break the captivity many find themselves in.

God has placed a plan into the physics of this world just for us. It is a marvel of love, an incredible feat of engineering, and a safety manual. Despite being born sinners, and born with an Adam-like nature which cannot enter the new heaven and earth, God loves us and does not give up on us until the last moment when Christ will return to take His bride. God teaches us how we can change our lives; shed the Adam-like nature for a Christ-like nature by learning about Him; what He asks of us, and how He will help us achieve this goal. But He also teaches us about Satan and why Satan must stop God from finding souls who choose to strive for righteousness rather than those things Satan wants for us so he can remain free.

Through His words in scripture God also teaches us how to avoid heartache, illness, and the dangers of sin, and teaches us how to prepare for various occurrences which scripture predicts will happen. Sadly, many challenge scripture and the value of placing our faith in God. They scoff at matters pertaining to faith or religion with a closed mind and heart. What scripture tells us about the end of those who continue in this mind set is horrific. Hell is horrific. Hell is for all eternity because the soul never dies.

This book is written to describe God's plan for mankind and how it relates to the heartache we face. It is to demonstrate why we fall into terrible circumstances and why it is so difficult to disentangle ourselves from them.

God wants all men saved and He tells us how we can be saved, even from Satan. Sadly, many do not know what God offers or what Satan does, and even more heartbreaking, many will not accept what God offers.... and soon it will be too late to escape what that decision will produce.

Scripture provides answers to all our questions and tells us that God has made equal provision for everyone who ever lived or died. It explains why Satan must work to break our faith and how he does this. Thus it addresses the addictions and sins we fall into which brings us into captivity to Satan. It is hoped that this book will provide the reader with an understanding of spiritual warfare, spiritual invasion and how these relate to addictions.

It addresses God's plan and His loving and consistent message.... and His words of warning.

We welcome your comments and your requests for the content of future books in this series. They are being written for those who seek and hunger but cannot find the time or energy to study the word of God. It is for all of us who want to connect to God, learn about Him, and to understand what God does for those who want to be prepared for the return of Christ. It is for those who desire to spend eternity with God.

Millions of people from every part of the world are currently being struck by the heartache of addiction and sadly, it will get worse, and be so bad that scripture tells us that if God did not shorten this time even His elect would be lost. It is for these battles that we need to understand what is occurring in the world of satanic power which forces Satan to bring us so much heartache, so much suffering and such incredible anxiety. We must make ourselves ready for Christ's return and can only accomplish this is if we know what God wants us to learn.

May God bless you and keep you and touch your heart with the desire to learn of Him and be free.

Helen Gumienny Glowacki

"Drop down ye heavens, from above,

and let the skies

pour down righteousness,

let the earth open,

and let them bring forth salvation,

and let righteousness

spring up together,

I the Lord created it."

Isaiah 45:8

TABLE OF CONTENTS

Photography by Colette van Loggerenberg

"And I will give you pastors

according to mine heart,

which shall feed you

with knowledge and understanding."

Jeremiah 3: 15

Chapter One

WHAT NO ONE WILL TELL YOU

Today's world is fraught with activities which often cause unintentional pain and suffering. This comes from a lack of understanding about the powerful enemy we face who wants to prevent us from becoming the Bride of Christ. Few understand, thus have not taught their children and youth about the meaning of one of the most important verses in the Bible. This verse is from Matthew 12:45 and says, *"Then goeth he, and taketh with him seven other spirits more wicked than himself, and they enter in and dwell there; and the last state of that man is worse than the first".*

Few people understand that an ongoing war exists between God and Satan and that we are the prize, we are those who inevitably must choose whether to fight on the side of good, or remain captive to the side of evil. Satan operates so clandestinely in our lives that we may not even be aware of the choice we have made until it is too late. Just as a hunter prepares a trap for his prey and the prey is surprised when it is captured, so does Satan work to trap us.

Satan is subtle, and has greater success when we are not aware of his work, nor aware that it can endanger our soul. He wants us to eliminate God from our life, forget what God tells us in scripture and wants us to die in that state of unawareness. He does not want us to learn that many of our attachments are to those things which are displeasing to God and which cannot be brought into heaven.

When Satan was thrown out of heaven because of his rebellion against God, he brought with him one third of all the angels. These had joined him in his fight against God. All of these beings have the ability to enter mankind and influence them. Each seems to have a "specialty" with which they plague mankind and provoke him toward behaviors which are displeasing to God. Two such behaviors which the verses in Matthew 12:45 warns of, are those causing drug and alcohol addiction. Yet society never informs us that such a possibility or that such a spirit even exists. Instead, society puts forth two philosophies about addictions which are misleading. One philosophy claims that addictions originate from a pre-birth disposition, and another claims that illness is the driving factor of an addiction.

Both these philosophies remove the onus of responsibility from the individual and imply the need for a greater tolerance. They also demand that all addictions be treated similarly. The flaw in this concept is that while society excuses some addictions, there are others it does not excuse such as kleptomania, pornography, anorexia, and pedophilia, to name a few.

Adam and Eve's sin was the initial act which caused all men to sin, and gave the spirits of this world access to us. Further, Scripture tells us that we can inherit, and suffer from, the sins of our forefathers. This may indicate that the same spirits which influenced our ancestors can also influence us. Jeremiah 11:10 says, *"They are turned back to the iniquities of their forefathers, which refused to hear my words;….."*. Exodus 20:5 says *".....visiting the iniquity of the fathers upon the children unto the third and fourth generation...."* And in Numbers 14:18, we are told *"....and by no means clearing the guilty, visiting the iniquity of the fathers upon the children unto the third and fourth generation."*

Thus, what our parents, grandparents, great-grandparents, or even relatives further back in time, engaged in could impact us. Accepting these passages at face value, the question which follows is: "At what point do we excuse a behavior on the basis that it occurs because of the sin of an ancestor, or because 'the devil made me do it'?" The answer must be: "At no point". We are and must remain individually responsible for what we do, for God teaches that we must strive to overcome everything within us which He cannot in His righteousness allow to enter His new kingdom.

Scripture teaches that we are to strive to escape the captivity Satan exercises over us in these matters if we want to be found worthy. Further, being aware of what scripture tells us becomes an incentive and a comfort to those engaged in, yet saddened by their activities, because scripture tells us that God will help us. While the world accepts, condones, and sometimes encourages certain behaviors, our duty is to learn what God tells us, avoid what displeases Him, and help others escape from the satanic captivity causing these behaviors. While many know of Adam and Eve and the inherited sin they brought to mankind, few understand how the sins of our ancestors can impact us. If these create a gene, pre-disposition, or illness which makes us susceptible to an addiction, we must learn what God says about how we are to overcome it. We must acknowledge that God in His righteousness cannot allow *any* evil, *any* sin into His kingdom because He wishes to protect the perfect love which He desires to reign in His kingdom.

Evidence indicates that drug users and alcoholics have overcome their addictions through programs which use the faith-based approach of abstinence. Why then should we succumb to the belief that we cannot overcome *all* addictions? If we can free ourselves of one destructive spirit, why should we not be able to free ourselves of any spirit through God's instruction? If, as some say, we inherit a kind of DNA change which allows a specific spirit to cause a thirst for something which is displeasing to God, and if we accept that the sin of Adam and Eve allowed Satan access to man, we should also accept that the sin of our forefather's also allows a satanic spirit access to us. However, whatever the cause, we must look to how God tells us we can fight back.

Matthew 8:16 explains that there were many possessed by evil spirits in Christ's time and that when Christ cast these spirits out, the people were healed. *"When the evening was come, they brought unto him many that were possessed with devils: and he cast out the spirits with his word, and healed all that were sick."*

Luke 8:29 says, *"(For he had commanded the unclean spirit to come out of the man. For oftentimes it had caught him: and he was kept bound with chains and in fetters; and he brake the bands, and was driven of the devil into the wilderness.)"* This verse explains that the spirit kept the man bound, and that the devil drove the man to do his bidding. However, through the power of Christ, through prayer and abstaining from those things which the spirit demanded, that spirit could be made to leave. Both abstinence and God's help to maintain that abstinence, is the key to overcoming these spirits.

The Bible clearly tells us that some spirits are more difficult to remove, but by prayer and fasting they can be made to leave. "Fasting" in this context means to "stay away" from, abstain from, the activities they require for their existence. Scripture teaches that when the apostles complained that they were unable to cast out a certain spirit, Christ told them that only by prayer and 'fasting' could they be cast out. Matthew 17:21 clearly states: *"Howbeit this kind goeth not out but by prayer and fasting."* And Mark 9:29 says, *"And he said unto them, This kind can come forth by nothing but by prayer and fasting."* These verses address the spirits and also why they would leave a soul. They "come forth" meaning...leave....through our prayers and by fasting or starving that spirit of what is desires.

We associate the word fasting with denying ourselves food, but here it clearly indicates that we must deny the spirit that which is requires to live, whether it is drugs, alcohol, pornography, or any other lust (spirit) we wish to be free of. While some spirits are easily rebuked, others cling to those whom they have invaded with incredible tenacity. By not "feeding" them, by abstaining from what they want and need to live, they have no choice but to leave! This requires that we run from temptation when it presents itself.... and stay away from that temptation. When that spirit finally starves because it cannot obtain what it wants, it will leave for a more satisfying experience through a more easily directed person. The bottom line is that some must fight a very powerful and tenacious spirit to become all that God wants them to become. Yet, God is willing to help; He knows the power of those spirits and He knows the striving of the heart.

Failure does not mean defeat; it means that we need to fight again, and that each time we fight we become stronger and more beloved of God. Therefore we should strive to overcome all addictions and all tendencies which we know are not pleasing to God and believe that, in time, those spirits can be broken and forced to leave.

Failure doesn't mean someone can't be forgiven or loved, or nurtured through the process of change, but it does mean that they cannot keep on believing that what they do is acceptable to God. A predisposition, the sins of their forefather's, an illness, a specific DNA, or even being wired a certain way does not excuse or condone the behavior. Proverbs 3:5 tells us, *"Trust in the Lord with all thine heart; and lean not unto your own understanding".*

God's words will always tell us the truth and always work to bring us into freedom. As children of God we need to understand the incredible connection between original sin, generational sin, and the spirits which attack and seek a home, in mankind. We need to talk about this subject and learn what scripture tells us. We need to be aware that Satan works feverishly to keep us from God and to hold us back from becoming the Bride of Christ.

It is important that we share this concept with others so we can **all** help those who desire to free themselves from those spirits which keep us from God. We must unite in this godly position, rather than fall into the complacency and acceptance of those things which may prevent us or someone we love from being one of the five wise virgins rather than one of the foolish, and lose their place in Heaven. If we do not understand what position we must take, we can't teach our children its importance. Thus many children may believe that they can 'dabble' in what is potentially incredibly dangerous to them and remain safe. They need to understand that this may open them up to a spiritual invasion that will not only ruin their lives, but prevent them from entering Heaven..

We all need to understand that spirits which enjoy the power of causing man to engage in those activities which are displeasing to God can enter someone and cause them to want more. Eventually that spirit will control them and force them to feed that spirit. They need to be taught that with *each* encounter with any of these addictions, the spirit will garner a stronger hold over them and become increasingly difficult to remove… and could cost them their soul salvation.

God leaves no question unanswered. Sadly, when parents don't have the answers, they can't teach their children, and without this knowledge children will succumb to these spirits. Many children…and adults….are not aware of what their children face in today's culture, and they don't know how to protect their children from these perils. This is why God asks us to know His words and to remain in constant fellowship with one another. Talking with one another about God's admonitions is crucial.

If we remain unaware of the power of Satan and his cohorts, or how easily we can become trapped, we cannot make an informed decision, understand the choices we have, nor the consequences of our actions. We must help our children and youth understand why they must say "NO" and ***flee*** from what has become acceptable in the eyes of the world… despite being displeasing to God. The world is too dangerous to our spiritual well-being for us not to be armed with God's warnings. We need to have the courage to stand up and fight for those principles and help others do the same.

As we bring our testimony however, it is important to exercise love and compassion, patience, instruction, and to pray for and with those who are trapped. When we stand firm in rebuking these spirits yet act with love and patience, the spirits which have trapped so many begin to weaken. If we remember the words, *"There but by the grace of God go I",* we will find that providing love, compassion, prayer, and exhortations about what God tells us in scripture will be the path to understanding. Godly wisdom helps us know where we must stand and how to help. Thus, most importantly we must learn from scripture, understand what we learn, and teach what we have learned, especially that Matthew 12:45 warns, *"Then goeth he, and taketh with him seven other spirits more wicked than himself, and they enter in and dwell there; and the last state of that man is worse than the first".*

Further, this same philosophy applies to homosexuality. This proclivity also claims a pre-birth disposition which removes the onus of responsibility from the individual. Again however this argument will not withstand the question of which addictions one must excuse on this basis and which we should not….and why the difference? If we consider homosexuality, alcoholism, and drug addiction acceptable on the basis of a pre-disposition or an illness, then why do we not remove the onus of responsibility from those engaged in kleptomania, pornography, gluttony, anorexia, and pedophilia, to name a few? Yet *all* these spirits, according to scripture, can be made to leave.

The Bible even more specifically addresses homosexuality. Romans 1:27, 32 says: "*And likewise also the men, having the natural use of the woman, burned in their lust toward one another; men with men working that which is unseemly, and receiving in themselves that recompense of their error which was meet. Who knowing the judgment of God, that they which commit such things are worthy of death, not only do the same, but have pleasure in them that do them."* Leviticus 18:22 says: *"Thou shalt not lie with mankind, as with womankind: it is abomination."* And Leviticus 20:13 tells us: *"If a man also lie with mankind, as he lieth with a woman, both of them have committed an abomination: they shall surely be put to death...."* 1 Corinthians 6:9 tells us, *"Know ye not that the unrighteous shall not inherit the kingdom of God? Be ye not deceived..... nor effeminate, nor abusers of themselves with mankind."* And, 1 Timothy 1:9-10 states: *"Knowing this, that the law is not made for a righteous man, but for the lawless and disobedient, for the ungodly and profane......for them that defile themselves with mankind....and if there be any other thing that is contrary to sound doctrine...."*

Further, Genesis 19:1-13 addresses the proclivities of the men of Sodom, the city God destroyed because of their sin and which is the basis of the word sodomy. There are additional passages in scripture which describe homosexuality as a sin before God and even warns us that this activity will increase as we near the First Resurrection.

God asks His children to strive to overcome *all* things which are displeasing to God. He is fully aware of how much we strive and how much we hate our sin. Scripture explains that if we fail, we must have remorse for that failure, and try again to overcome. We must never be complacent about our sins, large or small and must always desire to overcome them.

We need to understand that there is an incredible connection between original sin, generational sin, and unclean spirits which attack and dwell in mankind. We need to learn what scripture tells us and *unite* in the godly position we should take to combat this scourge rather than fall into the complacency and acceptance of those things which may prevent us or someone we love from being found worthy. Furthermore, if we see these sins and do not rebuke these sins we will also have to pay a heavy price. By *not* doing as God asks and by *not* helping others by accurately and completely sharing God's words, we are actually *supporting* the work of these spirits.

Only when we understand what position we must take, can we teach our children its importance and help them understand that they must not even 'dabble' in drugs, alcohol, homosexuality, or pornography. We all need to acknowledge the danger and that the spirit or spirits which enjoy those activities can enter man and create the need which leads to addiction. Eventually *those spirits will control and force* whomever it has entered to "feed" it what it craves. Thus our children need to be taught that with *each* encounter into *any* of these addictions, the spirit of addiction will garner a stronger hold over them and become increasingly difficult to remove.

Matthew 12:45 says, *"Then goeth he, and taketh with him seven other spirits more wicked than himself, and they enter in and dwell there; and the last state of that man is worse than the first".*

Bullet Points

- Many in today's society assign certain behaviors to illness or an inherent proclivity.
- Neither of these assignations allow that those behaviors are sinful or that one must strive to overcome them.
- Scripture designates that certain behaviors arise from satanic influence.
- Scripture also designates that inherited sin comes from satanic influence.
- God's words tell us how to remove and overcome both inherited sin and satanic influence.
- "Fasting" means to eliminate the access, influence and temptation a spirit demands.

Supporting Scripture

- Romans 1: 27, 32,
- Leviticus 18:22,
- Leviticus 20:13,
- Jeremiah 11:20,
- Exodus 20:5,
- Numbers 14:18,
- Matthew 12:45,
- Mark 9:29,
- Psalms 37:3,
- Proverbs 3:5,
- Luke 8:29,
- 1 Timothy 1:9-10,
- Genesis 19:1-13,
- 1 Corinthians 6:9,
- Matthew 8:16,
- Matthew 17:21

Photography by Matthew Burniston
Photo edit and verse overlay by Colette van Loggerenberg

Chapter Two

WHY TOUGH LOVE IS REAL LOVE

The term "tough love" became popular when its attributes were discussed by Bill Milliken in his book Tough Love which was published in 1968. These words became popular again in the 1980's when David and Phyllis York developed a set of strategies for employing tough love. These arose from the needs of those coping with the addictions of people they loved.

During these two eras, parents were surprised to learn that their children were using drugs and alcohol and were falling prey to other addictions as well. Initially the parents covered the transgressions of the child. But as children fell further into their addiction and lost touch with what they had been taught about Biblical principles, many parents recognized the need to intervene on a greater level.

Over time, studies were conducted and books written about how to overcome these addictions, and strategies were developed for those who sought help. Christians understood that indifferent disregard for right and wrong would damage one's soul salvation and sought assistance from their church by requesting counseling and intervention from their ministers.

As the behaviors of the addicted were further studied, the passive behavior of those seeking to help was also studied and brought forth astounding information. Studies demonstrated that many of those who interacted with someone with an addiction had fallen into the trap of wanting to be their “friend”, wanting to avoid confrontation and unconsciously seeking and needing their approval.

It became clear that this type of parenting and friendship contributed to the addiction of those they wanted to help and was thus proclaimed to be an “enabling” personality. This personality is one where the enabler “feels good” by believing they are providing love when they allow, support, and champion those with an addiction and even believe that they are following biblical precepts by doing so. Yet they are actually helping themselves because the undying devotion and adulation of those they enable feeds their personal needs and creates a co-dependency.

Through this co-dependency the enabler has his or her needs met, and the addicted exists in a relationship which comfortably contributes to their behavior. As long as the addict has their enabling devices in place, they can deny that what they are doing is wrong.

Newer studies determined that co-dependency is an addiction of its own and that the enabler has a fear of abandonment which causes them to become addicted to being needed and appreciated. They bask in what they consider their courage in standing up for others. They are often however, unconsciously acting out of an emotional wound or programming from childhood.

Real love is not selfish. It does not look for love in return. It looks for the well being of others and therefore to their relationship with God. Real love is willing to lose someone's adulation to help them understand what holds them back from being found worthy. Real love is supporting someone through their addiction without condoning it.

From a Christian perspective, *both* the addicted and enabling personalities need to be addressed. The captivity and destruction these behaviors produce must be acknowledged and broken. Destructive behavior is any behavior which is or results in displeasing God. Furthermore scripture tells us that anyone who causes or enables the stumbling of another is not pleasing to God and will be severely judged for doing so.

Matthew 18:6-7 tells us, *"But whoso shall offend one of these little ones which believe in me, it were better for him that a millstone were hanged about his neck, and that he were drowned in the depth of the sea. Woe unto the world because of offenses! For it must needs be that offenses come; but woe to that man by whom the offense cometh!"*

Further into this chapter God explains that He does not want these sheep to be lost, but that if an offense exists it must be "plucked out". It also tells us that **the "church" must explain their fault and help them overcome**. Thus by pretending that the "fault" is acceptable because it is an addiction is ungodly, and contributes to both parties failing to keep God's statutes.

Luke 17:1 also addresses this issue and says, *"....offenses will come; but woe unto him, through whom they come."*

Throughout scripture God tells us to rebuke the sinner, to overcome sin, and to seek forgiveness. It also teaches us that God looks for what lives in our heart, for our striving, and not at our failures. As we read about the sins of our forefathers and the "tendencies" one might have for any addiction, we know that God understands the struggle involved.

Scripture clearly tell us that God promises the strength to overcome, demonstrates that these spirits can be made to leave, and promises His grace for those who strive. His grace is extended to those who continue to fail but who have acknowledged their sin, hate their sin because of their love for God, and strive to the best of their ability to overcome it.

Nowhere in scripture does it say that God simply "excuses" sin or allows us to ignore, accept or justify it. Sin is sin, addiction or not, and can keep us from being found worthy. However, God forgives our sin and teaches us to forgive, not to judge, to love our brethren and bear their burdens as we rebuke the sin.

Romans 1:24 tells *us "Wherefore God also gave them up for uncleaness through the lusts of their own hearts, to dishonour their own bodies between themselves. Who changed the truth of God into a lie, and served and worshipped the creature more than the Creator...."*

Tough love offers a set of strategies which guide a parent or friend in setting boundaries with those they want to help. These include love, support, longsuffering, patience, and all the fruits of the spirit yet still rebuke and teach about the sin. This helps enablers move from their Adam-like fallibility of selfish need to the Christ-like nature which teaches to "go and sin no more". This also provides the sinner with help but never condones their sin, and in fact reminds them of God's help and their free will to choose to fight their sin... or lose their soul salvation. Harsh words, but true.

2 Timothy 4:2-4 tells us "*Preach the word: be instant in season out of season: reprove, rebuke, exhort with all longsuffering and doctrine. For the time will come when they will not endure sound doctrine; but after their own lusts shall they heap unto themselves teachers, having itching ears; and they shall turn away their ears from the truth, and shall be turned unto fables.*"

Sadly, the world in which we live has become a world of enablers under the guise of "political correctness". Thus, many are afraid to stand against sin and many have such a strong need to be tolerant that they unknowingly enable addictions so they can feel noble, loved, appreciated and needed.

Further, justification reigns in today's world and causes even Christians to convince themselves that they must never judge therefore must support those who cannot stop their sin. This however is enabling... and while real love does not judge or condemn, it does recognize sin and rebuke it with gentleness, kindness and by example.

Malachi 2:8 tells us, *"But ye are departed out of the way; ye have caused many to stumble at the law; .....".*

Luke 22:32 tells us, *"But I have prayed for thee, that thy faith fail not; and when thou art converted, strengthen thy brethren."*

God wants us to help one another, but to do so under *His* will and according to *His* precepts. The bride must be worthy of Christ and *no* evil or evil spirits can or will be allowed in God's kingdom. Our job is to strive to overcome all sin and to preach this to our brethren.

We cannot allow the political correctness of the day which preaches the tolerance and support of sin to guide our decisions. We must learn what God says and teach this so that we do provide the help which will ensure the soul salvation of those we wish to help.

All Christians, enabler or not, must learn how to stand strong for Biblical principles and reach out to teach those principles making no excuses for them. Offering tough love does not mean being cruel. The real cruelty is to enable and condone the sin, and thus mislead those who come to us for support.

Bullet Points

- Tough love offers a set of strategies which guide a parent or friend in setting boundaries.
- Enablers must move from their Adam-like fallibility of selfish need to the Christ-like nature which provides the sinner with help without condoning their sin.
- Enablers have a co-dependency which is an addiction of its own.
- Offering tough love does not mean being cruel.

- The real cruelty is to enable and condone the sin, and thus mislead those who seek support.

Supporting Scripture

- Matthew 18:6-7,
- Luke 17:1,
- Romans 1:24,
- 2 Timothy 4:2-4,
- Malachi 2:8,
- Luke 22:32.

Photography by Matthew Burniston
Photo edit and verse overlay by Colette van Loggerenberg

Chapter Three

<u>WHEN TO HOLD AND WHEN TO FOLD</u>

Witnessing the subtle control which evil exercises over those we love by creating spiritual blindness and stiff-necked resistance to God's words, can cause us to become frustrated. It also allows our well intentioned testimony to become a seemingly unproductive argument. When our prayers appear to go unanswered and we tire from the constant struggle of an interaction which seems to bears no fruit, we wonder if we should give up or increase our effort. But the truth is that knowing when to hold and when to fold and why we should do so are important factors for us to consider.

As children of God we desire to be kind, empathetic, and compassionate while also being strong, firm and have no fellowship with evil. Ephesians 5:11 tells us: *"And have no fellowship with the unfruitful works of darkness, but rather reprove them."* Yet in Galatians 6:2 we are told, *"Bear ye one another's burdens."*

On the surface these verses seem contradictory, but other parts of scripture show us that each has their place in how we bring testimony. Our life as children of God requires us to care for our spiritual life, the spiritual life of our family members, and to bring others testimony of God's plan of salvation and the sacrifice of Christ. To be effective we have to utilize God's teaching through scripture in word and deed, and to pray specifically about each situation we encounter. But we also have to act within the parameters of God's direction.

This requires the understanding that we are dealing with the power of Satan as well as our own Adam-like nature. When we fully understand that we battle powers and principalities which are the spirits of this world, we are not as easily discouraged by the unkind or ungodly words and deeds which our testimony might evoke nor of the appearance of a failed testimony.

Scripture teaches us that when we bring testimony to someone under satanic control, we are not dealing with only the person to whom we speak, but also with the spirit which holds them captive. That spirit considers the child of God a danger to its existence and is aware that their words and deeds have the power to remove them from the heart it has entered. That spirit will put up a fight to thwart all testimony and will direct its venom toward the person bringing that testimony. But the greater the attack, the more impact we are making on the soul.

Ephesians 6:10 tells us, *"....Be strong in the Lord, and in the power of his might."* Yet many times we allow our complacency to set in and make excuses about what we witness around us. God does not want us to do that, especially with another child of God. He asks that we teach, rebuke, admonish, support, help and love, but never to let God's children slip away from His truths.

When we acknowledge that we are not dealing with the person to whom we bring the testimony, but with the spirit which is determined to remain comfortably in their heart, we must ask God to help us discern when it is time to hold and hammer away, or time to fold and come back another day with our testimony.

It is imperative for the children of God to understand that by providing constant assistance to a soul, we may be aiding, abetting and enabling that spirit to thrive, rather than helping the soul rid itself of the spirit which impels the behavior which is displeasing to God. This is a very important point for all children of God to consider when engaging in testimony.

To be effective against these spirits we must understand the term "tough love" discussed in an earlier chapter. The tough love approach advocates that we carefully assess the assistance or interaction we provide to determine whether or not our intervention is aiding and abetting the harmful behavior of that soul. If so, we have become what is termed an "enabler". This term is often used when addressing those burdened by a drug addiction but apply equally for all behaviors which are not pleasing to God. Neither action of holding or folding indicates that we are winning or have given up. Both actions have a time and a place in our testimony, and both actions are godly.

It is not an either or situation when we hold and fold, but a combination which allows us to bring our testimony through word and deed (hold) while firmly refusing to enable (fold). The term to "hold or fold" is used in the card game of Poker to describe the decision to increase a bet in the hope of winning, or withdraw from further betting because one feels that they cannot win. Sometimes a bluff will create a win as well. Similarly, the child of God deciding to hold or fold is making the decision to provide testimony to the person in need while being careful to walk away before providing assistance to the spirit in control.

The spirit in control knows and fears those who recognize it and know its needs. When the child of God "holds" by identifying, rebuking and "starving" the spirit they are addressing, it will eventually look for greener pastures where it will not be identified and challenged.

However, we must walk away or fold when the soul allows the spirit to abuse us in word or deed. Once our point is made and the spirit is identified and rebuked, it can be told that we recognize its venom and will return at another time to speak with the soul. This disallows the spirit the freedom to use the soul to dispel its wrath. In time the soul recognizes the work of the spirit and begins to desire freedom and the spirit becomes aware that it will soon become displaced and may work even harder to stay. However, once this recognition takes place, the spirit can only fight back for a short period of time.

Amazingly, scripture tells us how a soul can cause an invading spirit to leave. Mark 9:29 tells us: *"This kind can come forth by nothing, but by prayer and fasting."* In this context the word fasting means denying or starving the spirit of what it desires. Once we have developed a full understanding of what God teaches us about invading spirits, we will no longer feel guilty when denying certain forms of assistance, nor be angered when meeting with resistance. We will no longer lose heart or think of giving up our testimony. While this infuriates the spirit, lets it know that it has been recognized, rebuked and will no longer be "fed" what it desires, it also knows that we will not give up.

When we face a spirit and know what scripture tells us about these spirits we are better armed to teach its victim to recognize it and thus understand why they are separated from God and how to free themselves. Once the soul acknowledges the spirit, the spirit knows its days are numbered, and our testimony begins to bear fruit even if we cannot see the progress being made. The spirit in control does not want the soul it has invaded to recognize it and rightfully fears those who do.

If that spirit sees that those bringing testimony has identified it and will "starve" its needs through tough love, it fears that the soul in which it lives will also recognize it, begin its fight against that spirit and with God's help overcome it. Thus it attacks the child of God bringing their testimony to that soul.

However, if we offer help as an enabler, that spirit will use us and not budge from its hold on the soul. It has no reason to leave, because you, the one who seeks to help, are enabling the spirit just as you are enabling the one you are seeking to help. We must offer our help yet remain firm in our faith and in testifying of God's laws and precepts for attaining our soul salvation. We want to be good teachers and good role models while standing firm in our conviction.

If we reach out with understanding to those who suffer and we fully support our faith by bringing them God's words...both the admonitions and the promises....we become a role model to them. We demonstrate love despite their failures and consistently teach about the sin, the spirits which bind them to that sin, and what God offers them and gain respect for our stedfastness.

Once we have developed a full understanding of what God teaches us about invading spirits, we will no longer tire of the failure of our testimony, nor of the failure of the invaded soul to fight that spirit. We will have the patience to persevere, and the wisdom to fight. To be effective we also have to pray specifically about the situation and have the soul which is in captivity also pray. These efforts combine to help us connect to the power of the Holy Spirit and obtain God's gifts of direction, thus act within the parameters of those gifts. We are also increasing the power of the Holy Spirit in the captive soul. When we have initiated these actions and trust God to do the rest we will not become discouraged by the unkind or ungodly words and deeds which our testimony might evoke nor of the failure which our testimony might appear to be.

We must be ready for the spirit to put up a fight and direct its venom toward us. That spirit can attack the child of God in many ways and be a danger both to the one bringing testimony and to the one receiving that testimony. However, once we are aware of this we can ask God for His protection and His help to stand firm through it.

The spirits we face can see this determination in us and begin to understand that it cannot attack us with guilt or fear, or by convincing us that we will lose the fight or be forced to give it up. They can see that we mean business, that we are not afraid to face them and that we will expose them to those we wish to help through God's words. That spirit also sees that we are applying God's words with Christian courage and perseverance.

When we know God's words and trust that He will be with us and that His power is far greater than the power of the spirit, we can rest assured that our testimony will never be in vain. As we make it known that we recognize the spirit and rebuke its actions, yet love the soul, that spirit is then forced to acknowledge that we know when to walk away and when to return.

It knows that we will return to fight another day when God has again prepared that soul for further testimony and weakened that spirits hold on them just a little bit more…. and will do so until it leaves!

Bullet Points

- We must learn what God tells us about the spirits which roam the earth to harm mankind.

- We must understand the power that these spirits have over man.
- When we understand the testimony God wants us to share, we help others by sharing what we have learned.
- Sharing what we know of God's plan of salvation and the work of Satan may require that we bring this testimony to those who have been invaded by an unclean spirit.
- Tough love is a term used to teach an enabler not to aid and abet a destructive spirit.
- An unclean spirit will resist and attack the Christian because it fears the testimony.
- We are not discouraged when we know that the attacks come from the unclean spirit, rather than from the soul thus understand why it responds with vehemence to our testimony.
- The Christian should both hold and fold but not give up.

Supporting Scripture

- Ephesians 5:11,
- Galatians 6:2,
- Mark 5:16,
- 1 Timothy 2:4-6,
- Mark 5:8,
- Ephesians 6:10,
- Hosea 4:6,
- Matthew 18:18,
- Mark 5:2,
- Mark 5:9

Photography by Matthew Burniston
Photo edit and verse overlay by Colette van Loggerenberg

Chapter Four

HOW TO TURN ANGER INTO A BLESSING

Everyone, good or bad, gets angry. God even gets angry. Christ too, once became so angry that He overturned the market tables inside the gates of the temple. There are differences however between feeling anger, expressing anger, and maintaining anger. Anger is a natural consequence of the Adam-like nature and as we move from the Adam-like nature to the Christ-like nature we learn…and desire… to control our anger. Initially, we *feel* anger, but feeling anger can move into expressing anger which comes in two forms; one is productive and the other negative.

Productive expression is when we calmly acknowledge, and explain, why we felt anger over a certain situation, and what we believe should be put into place to prevent the cause of that anger in the future. This helps us avoid the circumstances which *cause* anger and helps us communicate our feelings and our needs to those with whom we interact.

Negative expression occurs when we openly express our feelings in a manner which angers others and….. we offer no constructive explanation of, or methods for, preventing the cause of these feelings. A negative reaction demonstrates that we have not controlled our anger, have not directed it toward solutions based in love and respect, and that we do not actively seek resolution. This is detrimental to those around us and detrimental to our soul salvation.

The act of maintaining our anger is encouraged by Satan and must be overcome. However, the memory of what caused our anger may serve to keep us from harm, but the maintenance or harboring of anger works to cloud our judgment, prevent change and growth, and robs us of love. It also robs us of the ability to maintain the fruits of the Holy Spirit which strives to guide us toward the godly love expressed by Christ.

Harboring anger can also make us ill because it destroys our peace and creates anxiety, hate, and other detrimental emotions. It also means that we have not forgiven. Forgiving does not require us to forget, for it is the memories we retain of the troubles we encounter as a result of sin, which helps us learn to avoid sin and evil in the future. However, forgiving others is necessary to obtaining our own forgiveness through Holy Communion.

Our worthiness when taking Holy Communion is *dependent* upon either our forgiving others or sincerely *striving* to forgive others for the harm they caused. Thus, while few acknowledge this fact, it is possible to participate in Holy Communion yet not have it be effective thus the sins we committed will not be washed away.

When Christ was asked what the most important commandment was, he said that we should love God with all our being and love our neighbor as ourselves. God has granted grace to us *on the condition* that we take the sacrament of Holy Communion *worthily.*

God understands that sometimes we continue to feel the hurt caused by someone or some deed they committed which brought us harm. He therefore accepts our *honest* efforts to work toward forgiveness knowing that this effort may not produce results overnight but will eventually.

We therefore must look into our hearts to examine whether or not we have truly forgiven the soul even when remembering the deed. If we have not, then we can promote forgiveness in our heart through the powerful tool of prayer asking God to help us forgive, and asking for the peace which Christ said He gladly gives us.

God answers our prayers and gives us what we need to overcome. He wants us to be happy and wants us to learn from our mistakes. Therefore He asks that we do not condemn and judge the person who brought us harm and made mistakes as well. God has clearly stated that He will take vengeance *for* us and that our job is to forgive. Our worthiness depends on us doing so.

Our Heavenly Father is very protective of His children and will not allow evil to overcome us. He is also very protective of the kingdom which He builds for the future where the Bride will reign with His Son. Thus He will not and cannot, in His righteousness allow *any* sin to enter it. Nevertheless, because God looks on the heart, He knows what we think and feel.

We, on the other hand don't know what conditions exist in the person who brought us harm. They may not yet know God, they may be pawns in Satan's hands, they may have suffered abuse, or they may labor under the captivity of jealousy from which they cannot escape. Perhaps we have misinterpreted what they said or did. Thus God asks us to wait, to trust that He will handle their indiscretions, and asks that we forgive so ***we*** are not burdened by ***their*** faults and failings.

The beauty of reacting as God asks us is that He tells us that ***He will bless us*** for striving to behave in this manner. It is up to the other person to seek their own forgiveness from God and those they harmed and….. to make restitution for the harm they caused. If they don't seek forgiveness or try to make restitution, God will deal with them.

None of us can be found worthy if we do not obtain the forgiveness of our sins. Thus those who brought us harm must also obtain that forgiveness. This requires *their* remorse, *their* desire not to commit that sin again and *their* attempt to make restitution.

Christ brought His message in love and gentleness and then allowed His message to take root as men took that message home with them. We too can bring a message, but it must not be presented in a manner which will evoke anger. Scripture explains that in time the power of love and prayer, and of our personal example, can cause our message to take root. Psalm 133:1 tells us, *"Behold, how good and how pleasant it is for brethren to dwell together in unity!"*

But God also tells us that in time, our prayers can make a huge difference. This is why He asks that we pray for those who harm us. Our prayers can cause them to change their ways and to also change how they deal with us. This is a part of the miracle of prayer…..it is a mark of its incredible power and healing.

Being angry with someone who caused our suffering when God offers us a blessing for handling it correctly makes no sense. We receive something incredibly valuable by handling our anger correctly. Satan may inspire someone to hurt us, but **God can turn it into a blessing for us.**

This is one of the most magnificent miracles of our life of faith and those who harm us have no

idea of the gift which the harm they brought us can actually provide for us!

Once we learn how this process works, we can overcome a great deal. We can think of the blessing and the gain our soul can make when we strive to forgive and ask for peace over the matter. We can help ourselves *and* we can help others. We can stand firm when we are attacked knowing that God loves us and will create a miracle from our experience. Even if we fall prey to fear or anger temporarily, we can work out of it, rise above it and bring joy to the heart of God in the process.

Even more exciting is that when others have been deeply hurt, we can help them find peace by teaching them how God can turn that hurt into a blessing for them that will amaze them and show them how much God loves them.

Colossians 3:21 tells us: *"Fathers, provoke not your children to anger, lest they be discouraged."* Hebrews 13:6 tells us: *"So that we may boldly say, The Lord is my helper, and I will not fear what man shall do unto me"*. Hebrews 13:16 tells us: *"But to do good and to communicate forget not; for with such sacrifices God is well pleased."* Matthew 7:12 tells us: *"Therefore all things whatsoever ye would that men should do to you, do ye even so to them...."* And Proverbs 16:24 tells us: *"Pleasant words are as a honeycomb; sweet to the soul, and health to the bones."* Proverbs 8:32 tells us: *"....for blessed are they that keep my ways."*

Anger has its place and sometimes we must be angry. But in most cases we become angry over something that doesn't really matter or something which will soon right itself. Scripture teaches us that the bottom line is to flee from evil, but love the soul, and where possible, keep peace with one another. We must work together to learn and teach God's words so we can be a part of the First Resurrection, and we must overcome the traps Satan lays for us.

However, some people are governed by evil and they are best left to God to handle. Some are so arrogant that they would never consider that what they do is wrong. But we must consider that there is the possibility that if we refuse to forgive someone and retain our anger toward them, it could be that God has answered *their* pleas for forgiveness and ***they will have our place at the wedding feast because of our inability to forgive.***

What is imperative is that we overcome the tendency to make a blanket judgment about what others do. Scripture teaches us to love one another, care for one another, and forgive one another, but not to judge one another….that is up to God alone. Our job is to continually examine with honesty if we are doing what God asks of us. We are to let our anger go and to forgive all harm even if we must remember it to protect ourselves in the future.

While we might be better served to avoid interaction with those who are governed by evil, God asks that we always forgive the soul because only He… not we… know what causes that soul to sin. If we strive to do as He asks, He promises to look after everything else. It is not easy to pray for those who brought us harm, but if we do, and if we ask God to help us to it, we find that it becomes easier each time and that our personal peace is restored. Then we find that those for whom we pray are less apt to harm us again and may even change the way they treat us entirely.

Nothing is hidden from God and every good thing we do touches His heart and brings us a blessing.

"For God shall bring every work into judgment, with every secret thing whether it be good, or whether it be evil." Ecclesiastes 12:14

Bullet Points

- When we handle our anger correctly God provides us with an amazing blessing.
- We can better understand the many faces of anger when we understand our Adam-like nature.
- God asks us to control both the anger and the hurt we feel when someone harms us.
- Our experiences help us learn how to help others deal with the hurt they feel from similar experiences.
- God promises to deal with those who bring us harm.
- God asks that we leave vengeance to Him.

Supporting Scripture

- Psalm 133:1,
- Colossians 3:21,
- Hebrews 13:6,
- Hebrews 13:16,
- Matthew 7:12,
- Proverbs 16:24,
- Proverbs 8:32,
- Ecclesiastes 12:14

Photography and verse overlay
by Colette van Loggerenberg

Chapter Five

WHAT ABOUT LIFE AFTER DEATH?

When we think of death we think of the cessation of life and the end of all function. Even if we believe in the eternal life of a soul, we think of it as something which may float or travel, something ethereal, but not as existing with the ability to think or feel or speak. Rarely do we associate the soul with a functioning system in any way similar to what we now have. Yet scripture describes life after death as having many of these attributes.

Hospitals can monitor the activity of the brain and use its data to pronounce the presence or absence of activity thereby having the authority to state when the brain has died. Sometimes the body continues to function with life supports systems, but for all intents and purposes life is considered over when a monitor tells us that brain function ceases to exist. While the human mind is an amazing creation which can operate like a well programmed computer, it also has the sensitivity of emotion and reason. Thus, it is fascinating to study what scripture tells us about life after death. The story of the rich man and of the beggar at his gate, who both died on the same night and were both buried, is incredibly indicative of how the mind continues to exist after death despite what hospital monitors may tell us. This story is found in Luke 16:19-31 and is spoken by Christ Himself. It describes the torment and concern of a rich man who finds himself in one realm of eternity, while the beggar finds himself in comfort in another realm across a gulf, and is in the company of Abraham who had found favor with God.

"There was a certain rich man, which was clothed in purple and fine linen,
and fared sumptuously every day. And there was a certain beggar named Lazarus
which was laid at his gate, full of sores. And desiring to be fed with the crumbs
which fell from the rich man's table: moreover the dogs came and licked his sores.
And it came to pass, that the beggar died,
and was carried by the angels into Abraham's bosom; the rich man also died,
and was buried: And in hell he lift up his eyes, being in torments,
and seeth Abraham afar off, and Lazarus in his bosom. And he cried and said,
Father Abraham, have mercy on me, and send Lazarus
that he may dip the tip of his finger in water, and cool my tongue for I am tormented

in this flame. But Abraham said, Son, remember that thou in thy lifetime
receivedst thy good things, and likewise Lazarus evil things; but now he is comforted,
and thou art tormented. And beside all this, between us and you there is a great gulf fixed;
so that they which would pass from hence to you cannot; neither can they pass to us,
that would come from thence. Then he said, I pray thee therefore, father,
that thou wouldst send him to my father's house. For I have five brethren,
that he may testify unto them, lest they also come into this place of torment.
Abraham saith unto him, They have Moses and the prophets; let them hear them.
And he said, Nay father Abraham; but if one went unto them from the dead,
they will repent. And he said unto him, if they hear not Moses and the prophets,
neither will they be persuaded, though one rose from the dead."

In these thirteen verses, Christ Himself describes the rich man as crying, asking questions, voicing his concerns, pleading, expressing agony, receiving, processing and responding to the answer he receives from Abraham. The rich man is in torment, burning and thirsting from the flames within his location.

Christ depicts the beggar as carried by angels to rest with Abraham and describes him as being comforted. Despite seeing the comfort and company in which the beggar Lazarus finds himself, the rich man demands that Lazarus continue to act as his servant and be sent to advise his brothers. This indicates his continuing arrogance. Other areas of scripture also describe a place for those who have died which contains different realms in which souls enter either to await the First Resurrection or languish in past sins. Scripture also tells us that we are to pray for these souls and that they may be hungering for an invitation to the Altar of grace. While that decision is up to God, we are to exercise loving compassion for all of mankind.

What many churches do not teach is that Christ entered hell after His death to bring the news of His triumph over death through His perfect sacrifice and that He remained there for three days. Scripture also tells us that when Abraham learned of Christ's triumph he rejoiced. John 8:56 tells us that Christ said, *"Your Father Abraham rejoiced to see my day and he saw it and was glad."*

Abraham had died long before Christ spoke these words and Christ had not yet provided the sacrifice that He was to make. Christ tells those to whom He was speaking that He knew Abraham before He, Christ came to earth, again inferring that life goes on after death. Further, Christ says that Abraham saw "His day" or His triumph which made Abraham, though he was dead, rejoice. Thus there is a great deal which scripture teaches us about life after death and about the return of Christ. From it we can also learn what those who are still living can do to help in God's work.

We also learn what happens to those who die in sin and what happens to them when Christ returns. We can learn what will occur in these realms when grace is removed from the earth and when Satan is bound and then loosed again. Scripture also tells us that God wants all men to be saved and that He knows why men sin and what circumstances existed for them that may have caused them to sin. Thus, only He can judge someone's sin and can and does offer grace as He sees fit, not as man deems it proper.

Scripture tells us to pray for those who have died and offer our help to souls who were either never taught or faced circumstances beyond their control and thus we should not judge them. God also understands the struggles of souls who had to deal with the inherited or generational sin which may have stalked them and which gave Satan an opening from which to attack and capture them. This is most evident today where we find so many souls trapped by the effects of drug addiction. Sadly, few understand the activities of Satan and few understand how they can participate in helping those who died under these circumstances and to whom God wants to offer grace.

Scripture demonstrates the all encompassing plan which God has instituted for mankind and the purity of the love He has for mankind which we can barely fathom. It also demonstrates why we cannot judge, why God has compassion for sinners and those who died in their sins, and what He wants us to do to help bring His plan of salvation to fruition. Scripture also shows us what we will face as we enter into the final stages of the war between God and Satan when Satan fills the earth with evil and cruelty prior to his defeat and breaks the faith of many. Scripture explains that we are the pawns Satan attacks and to whom God offers every protection until the spiritual war in which we are engaged is ended. God looks at the striving which lives in our heart, not at our failures. He looks for us to hate our sin and work to overcome it. He looks for those who will be an asset in His kingdom because they yearn to love and to live in righteousness and desire with all their heart to spurn all evil.

God also tells us that He will be gracious to those to whom HE chooses to be gracious. This further indicates that God sees into us, into our secret thoughts, and knows whether or not we are sincere…and that if we are, He does all He can to help us and to forgive us. However, Satan uses our addictions to keep us away from God. His goal is to prevent us from obtaining Holy Communion and thus the forgiveness we require. Satan is a strong and powerful force, thus many addicts no longer attend church services nor receive Holy Communion. Thus, our bearers of blessing have been imbued not only with power, but also with a great responsibility to teach, support, comfort, forgive…and rebuke….and always to love and set an example. Thus they should become a resource through which we learn, and pray and receive our soul care. **If we seek these gifts which God provides, it is also a sign that we have not given up, that we still strive and that we *desire* to overcome. These activities can weaken the spirits which have us trapped.**

Many addicts exist in eternity and are in great torment. Many have lost all desire to learn of God. Many who have died under the influence of drugs could be lost forever because it is more difficult to escape Satan's captivity when we enter into eternity and exist where there are only other addicts. As we said, God loves us and is longsuffering and forgiving and wants all men to be saved. However, all men will *not* be saved thus the addict needs to cling to the altar of grace with all the strength they can muster despite *any* failures they may have encountered. God knows everything and will know what lives in the heart and reward the *striving* of that heart and the love for Him which is found in that heart. If this is missing from our lives, there is no guarantee that we can be forgiven. But if we cling to our faith despite our failures, and do our best to practice that faith, God will not forget us in eternity. **Failure is not a reason to give up the altar, our prayer life, seeking the forgiveness of our sin, nor developing a close relationship with our bearer of blessing.**

Failure is not a reason to give all to Satan. Even when it appears that Satan is winning the fight regarding the lusts of the body, it is still necessary to control the fight for the soul. When God sees us fight, and pray and strive....the reward will be ours. **Repeated failure does not mean that success is not around the corner.** With every prayer, and every connection to the altar the addictive spirit is weakened and forced to consider locating another heart to invade where it can be safe and comfortable. Making life unbearable for that spirit means that in time ***you*** will win the battle.

Bullet Points

- God looks for our striving and whether or not we cling to the altar of grace.

- God gives us those who will help us overcome.

- Failure does not mean that God no longer loves us.

- Trying again always touches God's heart.

- Studying God's words help us learn how to use all He offers us to have a better life

- Reaching out to help others always touches God's heart

Supporting Scripture

- Luke 16:19-31,
- John 8:56,
- Ecclesiastes 12:14,
- Proverbs 8:32,
- Mark 9:29,
- Matthew 12:45

Photography by Matthew Burniston
Photo edit and verse overlay by Colette van Loggerenberg

Chapter Six

WHAT DOES GOD WANT ME TO KNOW?

God wants us to learn, through His words in scripture, about His plan of salvation, the enemy we fight, our potential future, and how to prepare to become a part of the Bride of Christ. That preparation requires us to learn of the love He has for us and the love we are to develop within ourselves so we can meet the requirements He has set forth for our life in His new kingdom. When we do learn of the incredible plan which He placed into our world, the future He desires for us, and how to attain it, we can understand why only the purest of love will reign in the new kingdom and that no evil will exist.

Love is the decision to seek the well being of others before ourselves and it is what God wants us to develop so we can become the Bride of Christ. Practicing the love of giving and of self-sacrifice demonstrates that we are prepared for the society which God wants to institute in the new heaven and earth.

God Himself is the personification of perfect love. Love includes loving ourselves.... and this requires us to respect the temple which our bodies must become for the indwelling of the Holy Ghost who teaches us, guides us, and protects us.

God also wants us to learn that He wants to help us and has provided many avenues for us to access that help. He loves us far more than we can fathom and wants to prepare us for everything we will face....

including the difficulties Satan brings us and which His plan of salvation and righteousness requires we experience. He wants us to have the information with which to make our choices and our preparations, and to develop the trust in Him which will help us endure the difficulties which we will encounter. **He wants us to know how to recognize and fight Satan.**

When we are faced with what seems a complex question, scripture can provide the answer. We need only to ask and God will help us understand His message. But we must trust Him and can only accomplish this when we have developed a close relationship with Him. We begin to know God by learning His words and placing them in our heart. Arming ourselves with complete trust in God's help allows the mysteries of scripture to unfold and provide us with direction for gaining the strength and the understanding which we require.

Truly knowing God provides us with the confidence to formulate bold questions and to locate answers which may have been previously hidden. **God unveils His truths as we are ready to accept them or as we need them.** However, life often brings troubles and heartaches, and it brings failure.

Sadly, when love, family, health, shelter or sustenance is threatened, we often blame God for our troubles and wonder why we are here, to what purpose we were born, and where we can find the help we need. For some, troubles also cause them to question the power and existence of God and can shake their faith.

To avoid the loss of our faith, especially during the end times when all children of God will be in travail, God wants us to learn that we can trust Him. By being recognizing and preparing for Satan's attacks, by understanding God's plan of salvation, and developing a close relationship with God we learn to trust Him and no matter what comes our way…to cling to Him and to our faith. Whether we die before, or we live to experience the coming of Christ, if we understand how and why Satan seeks to break us and thereby break our faith, we can be prepared. Our trust in God will be strengthened and our struggles will be rewarded.

To this end, God moved the hearts of men toward seeking and serving Him. To help us in this goal He inspired the writing which we know today as the Bible. It is from these writings that we learn why evil seeks to destroy mans relationship with God and that a war is being waged for our soul. We learn that by keeping man away from God, Satan remains free and can temporarily avoid what he knows scripture predicts as his end. We also learn about the power of spiritual invasion and captivity.

The miracle of scripture is that as we seek to understand, and come to God with a pure heart, His plan for us opens itself up and provides us with the answer to our questions. It draws us closer to God and is the rock upon which we can build our spiritual strength to fight against Satan. Knowing God's words and utilizing the gift brought by Christ creates the foundation of faith we require and the desire to work toward developing ourselves for the loving society which God plans for His new heaven and earth.

Scripture teaches us about death and life after death so we can understand grace and the consequences of allowing evil to capture our soul. Scripture describes both the torment and the joy which our life's choices will bring us when we die. It teaches us that the soul lives *forever* and that our choices determine where and under what circumstances our soul will exist *for all eternity.*

It also teaches that Christ brought salvation and the forgiveness of sin to those who died before He could make that sacrifice for them *and* for those who were either trapped against their will or did not receive instruction. Scripture clearly says that God sees all things and looks at our heart to determine our worthiness. Thus man cannot pretend to excuses to allow or be forgiven their sins, nor judge others. What scripture teaches helps us recognize the enormity and all encompassing nature of God's plan. It helps us understand the level of love which lives in God's heart for mankind and also the exquisite planning He developed and then executed on our behalf. But to fully understand scripture we must trust in its words, its direction and its warnings. Further, scripture teaches us that the soul never dies. It is eternal. Thus, what happens *after* death should be of great concern to everyone.

The first death occurs to everyone and is when our natural bodies die. But it is the second death which will occur to those who *cannot* be found worthy to live with God when His of plan of salvation is completed that is the most frightening. These souls will be sent to the Lake of Fire with Satan after judgment. This death brings about a separation from God which is final and eternal. God wants us to understand this and strive to avoid this at all costs. Thus **despite our errors, our failures, our sense of despair, we must always cling to the altar, and always seek forgiveness.**

Scripture also warns that during the time just prior to the return of Christ, we must live through the tribulations of the end times. Scripture clearly states that even the elect of God will suffer great temptation and tribulation at that time and that many will lose their faith and their soul salvation. We will be tested when we move through our most difficult moments when all children of God will encounter great difficulty, and we will feel that evil appears to have the upper hand.

Many will ask where God is as they witness evil thriving and good destroyed. They will cry to God and for help and expect an answer and expect immediate help. Unless they understand God's plan, they may believe that God is not helping and that evil will always win as it fights all good. Satan wants all men to believe that there is no God and give up.

Satan watches the children of God knowing that if they lose their faith by losing their connection to the altar, they will lose God's protection, and their part in the First Resurrection. This is **Satan's primary goal....not to create an addict, but to create someone who he can take from the altar through their addiction.** Our free will and God's righteousness which demands He allow us to exercise our free will, requires us to choose God's way, trust Him and endure in and through that trust until Christ returns. It requires that **despite our failures, we continue to *strive* to overcome.**

Satan knows that God desires a certain number of souls to create the Bride He seeks for His Son, and that by reducing that number, he will remain free to wreak his power over mankind. But God is all powerful and all knowing and if we understand His plan, we know that He will win the war which Satan has waged. What God is gaining during this battle is not only perfected souls for His new kingdom, but also the absolute defeat of evil. Once Satan has exercised everything which is available to him in the battle against goodness and righteousness, and must acknowledge that he cannot break the faith of the children of God, he too must acknowledge that God won this war through perfect righteousness. He can never say that he didn't know what he did was wrong, nor claim that God won by default or by force. He too must acknowledge that God won the war… and our souls…. through sheer righteousness and the power of love.

Thus we must learn through scripture that God's righteousness and perfection is and never will be compromised and that **our free will must be used to choose love and righteousness over evil** and hate. All people and even all evil must acknowledge and bow under that fact. Understanding this battle and developing the love, trust, and righteousness to fight and defeat evil will help us when we go through our trials and tribulations. Thus, despite our troubles and our mistakes and our failures, we must **stay close to God, to His altar of grace, ask for forgiveness** and …. endure. We must accept what occurs around us, while we fight our sin, and trust God to bring us through our tribulation no matter how long it seems to take or how difficult it is to endure.

It is important that we trust scripture. As we learn of God's plan of salvation and that God wants us to succeed in becoming worthy to live with Him for all eternity we can begin to understand who God is and what lives in His heart. We must also learn that there is a *powerful* entity afoot who does not want us to understand or believe what we read or even read scripture at all. He has the power to cause confusion, complacency and disbelief and has the power to pervert the true meaning of scripture. He works to discourage us and keep us from the altar of grace.

Satan knows that as long as he can prevent us from believing and from teaching others what we have learned, it will also prevent God from obtaining the number of faithful souls He longs for. Therefore, learning about Satan, and what he can… and does… do is important. Studying scripture is imperative, but *believing* what we read and *taking heed* of what we read can make the difference in whether or not we can be found worthy.

Satan knows that his last chance to break the faith of the Bride of Christ will occur during the end times. Since scripture warns us that he will do everything in his power to break our faith, we must be prepared by learning what we can do to ease the troubles, doubt and fear we will face….and to continue in our striving to stay closely attached to the altar.

The end times will be a time where our faith will be sorely tested for scripture tells us that God will not intervene when we think He should. Thus, preparing to be ***found*** worthy upon our natural death is as important as preparing to ***stand*** worthy during the difficulties we will experience.

As mentioned in an earlier chapter, the story of the rich man and the beggar, of whom Christ speaks in Luke 16:19-31, describes a beggar who died and was buried, and found himself carried by angels to Abraham's bosom. The rich man died, was buried, opened his eyes to great torment, found himself in hell, and asked that the beggar warn his brothers. He was told that they would not listen because like him, they had been given Moses and the prophets who explained this to them but that they "hear not".

This is a similar situation to what we are experiencing today. We have been provided with scripture which is the direct word of God through which we receive the warnings and instruction we require. Additionally, we have been given an enormous array of teaching tools which explain what scripture tells us……and still many do not listen.

Luke 17: 26-32 tells us that people ate, drank, married and were living life when the flood came, and Genesis chapter 18 and 19 tells us the same occurred when Sodom and Gomorrah was destroyed. They did not heed God's warnings and scripture tells us that it will be the same when Christ returns. People will be so busy living life that they will not have prepared for what scripture clearly tells us will occur. They will not only die because of it, but may also lose their soul salvation.

Christ tells is in Luke 17:34-36 that of two people working or sleeping, one will be taken and the other left behind. Matthew 25:1-13 is the parable of the ten virgins. This analogy likens the ten virgins who waited for the bridegroom to us as Christians who await the return of Christ and warns us that only five of the ten will be taken. These parables tell us that only half of those who believe they are ready will be properly prepared and actually taken.

Further, Matthew 24:21 describes the time in which we live with the words *"For then shall be great tribulation, such as was not since the beginning of the world, to this time, no nor ever shall be."* And Matthew 24:22 tells us, "*And except those days should be shortened, there should be no flesh saved, but for the elects sake those days shall be shortened.* Christ also commented upon these days in Matthew 24:15 saying, *"When ye therefore shall see the abomination of the desolation spoken of by Daniel the prophet, ..."* And Matthew 24:13, *"But he that shall endure unto the end, the same shall be saved."*

Thus the comparison between being prepared for the natural body to die and preparing for the difficulties which engulf us is very similar. If we are not prepared we will not stand firm when we are assaulted....and will not be found worthy. Christ also commented on the blessing which comes as a result of understanding what is required to be prepared when we read in Luke 10:23:, *"He turned him unto his disciples, and said privately, Blessed are the eyes which see the things that ye see."* And to those who do love and exercise their trust in God, scripture tells us in Revelation 2:9, *"I know thy works, and tribulation..."* And in Revelation 2:10, *"Fear none of those things..."*

Trusting God is a process which grows as we exercise our faith and God shows Himself to us. Scripture tells us that we will need a strong faith and great trust and patience when Satan attacks. But if we simply **never lose touch with the altar of grace despite what happens in our life,** Revelation 2:13 tells us *"I know thy works, and where thou dwellest, even where Satan's seat is; and thou holdest fast my name, and hast not denied my faith...."* And Revelation 2:26, *"And he that overcometh, and keepeth my works unto the end, to him will I give power over the nations."*

Interestingly, scripture also tells us in Revelation 7:13 that when the Bride is brought to heaven after Christ gathers them for the First Resurrection, an elder asks, *".....What are these which are arrayed in white robes? And whence come they?* Scripture answers this question in Revelation 7:14 through the words, *"....**These are they which came out of great tribulation, and have washed their robes, and made them white in the blood of the lamb**.* And Revelation 7:16 tells us, *"They shall hunger no more, neither thirst any more...."*

What these verses combine to tell us is that when our trials become terribly heavy and yet our hearts still hunger and thirst for God, we are developing into those who Christ will take when He returns.

We are "overcoming" the suffering by remaining firm in our faith, and thus when Christ comes He will wash away our sins and take us with Him to heaven. Scripture could not make any plainer what we will go through and what we must do to prepare.

Scripture also tells us not to fear these things but to expect them....fight them....prepare for them by always clinging to the altar.

Bullet Points

- We must learn what God says in order to do as He asks.

- There is life after death where the consequences of how we lived our lives will be felt.

- God offers us forgiveness even if we fail as long as we cling to the altar of grace and strive to overcome.

- The end times will bring all the children of God a great test of faith.

- Staying faithful will be difficult when God does not step in to intervene when God's children are persecuted.

Supporting Scripture

- Matthew 24:13,
- Matthew 24:15,
- Matthew 24:21,
- Matthew 24:22,
- Luke 10:23,
- Luke 16:19-31,
- Luke 17:34-36,
- Revelation 2:9-10,
- Revelation 2:13,
- Revelation 2:26,
- Revelation 7:16

Photography by Matthew Burniston

Photo edit and verse overlay by Colette van Loggerenberg

Chapter Seven

WHAT SHOULD I DO?

There are two very separate yet equally important things which scripture tells us about the coming tribulation. The first is that we must prepare spiritually to be found worthy. The second is that we develop such a strong trust in God that when we see evil appear to win, we will not lose our faith.

To accomplish these goals, we must learn of God by developing a close and intimate relationship with Him through knowing His words and doing our part to fulfill His plan of salvation. We must develop and practice love, and spurn evil. As we do these things, we will also learn that God is with us and that He will be with us right to the end of days despite what we see around us.

To allow us to approach God despite our sin, God graciously provided us with three sacraments which break the captivity created by our sins. These sacraments are Holy Baptism, Holy Communion and Holy Sealing and these are formal acts which God created for mankind for the sanctification of body, soul and spirit. They are processes which create a covenant with God whereby we can be made holy by removing what separates us from God and provide us with what we need to become a child of God.

A covenant is an agreement which creates a link between God and man and can be effected by those to whom God has endowed the power to do so. These recognize mans imperfection and his desire to be forgiven, and they break Satan's hold over us thus allowing us to have fellowship with God. The forgiveness of sin occurs *only* if we partake worthily. This means honestly acknowledging our sins, having true remorse for committing our sins, truly striving never to repeat those sins again, forgiving others, and making restitution where we can. God sees all. He knows our heart and He knows whether or not we really do make the effort to meet this criteria.

Holy Sealing is the act of administering the comforting presence, enlightenment and guidance of the Holy Spirit into our soul to help us understand scripture and desire to do those things which are pleasing to God. To be eligible to receive Holy Sealing one must have been baptized, must have obtained the forgiveness of their sins, which includes acquired faith and an acknowledgement of their desire to follow Christ, and agree to be one of God's family. Parents can give this word for their children if the parents agree to provide the child with spiritual teaching and activities. Scripture admonishes us that the greatest and *only unforgiveable sin* is to sin against the Holy Ghost.

Matthew 12:31-32 explains, *"....but the blasphemy against the Holy Ghost shall not be forgiven unto men."* Mark 3:29 tells us, *"But he that blaspheme against the Holy Ghost hath never forgiveness, but is in danger of eternal damnation."* The Holy Ghost is the teacher and guide for God's children and **cannot** dwell in a sinful heart. Thus it is important that we understand the sanctity and impact of these sacraments and not take them lightly.

We must never enter into these covenants with God or give our vow without our true desire to put forth *the effort* to learn and follow. Further, our relationship with God must be nurtured and become strong so that we can stand firm in our trust in God and in *striving* to spurn what is evil, thus allowing the Holy Ghost to dwell with us.

But there is another component to learning and understanding God's words, His plan and our willingness to heed those words. This is the requirement that we teach others, and share what we have learned and experienced with others. We do this because we have understood the true meaning of love and love demands this sharing. This, along with the strength of our faith and our trust in God will be tested during the time of tribulation when Satan becomes desperate to break our faith.

We are currently witnessing incredible unrest and calamity in the world. Killing without remorse and the killing of Christians is not only occurring world-wide, but is being condoned, and there are few places where one can find true peace and freedom. Thus many believe that we are in that time frame which scripture describes as the opening of the third seal and is addressed in Revelation 6:5-6, The description of these times provided in Revelation 6:5-6 of the releasing of this third seal depicts a man sitting on a black horse holding a pair of balances in his hand. Many theologians believe that this could imply the redistribution of wealth which many politicians openly embrace. It could indicate our current worldwide economic situation which points to a monetary collapse which could cause severe inflation, shortages of food and other important and necessary commodities.

Scripture tells us that there will be six "seals" opened and released upon the earth before Christ comes for His bride. Thus, the children of God will be required to live through these times. God, in His infinite love and kindness warns us through scripture about what is to come. He knows that by understanding what is to come**, we can prepare** and limit the effects of these occurrences. Therefore, just as Noah was warned about the coming flood and prepared when others did not heed the warning, and Joseph was warned about the famine which was to come and last for nine years and prepared while others did not, we are being warned about these end times.

Scripture clearly indicates that we are to apply its words to our present time and to learn from them what will help us endure these prophesied circumstances. **This includes the attack on our youth through the addictions which Satan encourages.** No one however, can explain in detail nor with any complete assurance everything that will occur and when. But many find serious direction and warning in scripture about the times in which we live and are heeding those words. It will be up to us to believe and to heed these verses as a warning and to prepare.

While we may not know the time frame or the duration of time for our greatest tribulations, we can decide if scripture is indicating that the return of Christ and the tribulation is imminent and whether or not we wish to prepare. If one does believe that these words of scripture mimic what we see happening in the world and do wish to prepare, **the first thing that is required is to prepare spiritually**. Examining our personal relationship with God, our level of faith and trust and what those we love may need spiritually, we can move to correct our shortcomings. Despite what may come, our spiritual state is the most important asset we can develop. Without a firm faith, we cannot endure and thus cannot become part of the Bride of Christ. Once our spiritual life appears intact, we can move to examining what we can do to improve our physical well-being and the physical well-being of those we love.

Many are concerned about the unrest we are witnessing world-wide, the poor economy which threatens a collapse of our monetary system, the weather and pestilence which cause crops to fail and food to become scarce, and the increase in sickness and natural disasters that have struck. Further, **we witness the scourge of addictions which Satan**

uses to separate our youth from God and the altar of grace.

These concerns have inspired many to learn how to prepare in every way they can and encourage parents to teach God's words to their children. Taking God's words to heart has encouraged some to grow their own food, purchase seeds for a garden which can produce food, stockpile dried food products or canned products and staples such as rice which has a long shelf life.

Others have converted their currency to a commodity recognized and accepted as holding its value and easily traded… such as gold and silver. **Many work in the vineyard to care for the souls trapped by Satan and help them understand the importance of the altar of grace and forgiveness and the short amount of time for preparing their soul for the return of Christ.**

Many are strengthening their faith so they can uplift others when fear and a loss of faith envelopes them. Many are praying that God will teach them and help them to trust and to be an example and support to others.

But what we also need to consider is that when these times come, Satan, who knows scripture far better than we do, also knows that his freedom will soon end. He knows that when God finds the number He longs for, He will send Christ and three and one half years later Satan will be bound. Therefore **Satan is *now* striking with greater vengeance than ever before. He has chosen a venue by which he can prevent our children from seeking God.** He believes that by breaking them he might prevent the next generation from seeking God.

Drugs and alcohol can easily prevent those trapped in these addictions from seeking God. **Whether it is the drugs themselves, or the guilt of the soul,**

or their submission to the spirit, the goal of Satan is to use these addictions to prevent the soul from seeking God and therefore seeking the forgiveness of their sins.

This plan is to reduce the number of souls God can claim as a part of the bride of Christ. It is for this reason that all Christians must reach out to these souls and teach them what is at stake and teach them that **if they cling to the altar and strive to overcome, God can forgive them and will help them.**

Therefore if we are looking for a plan of action by which we can be assured of God's love and protection *despite* our sins, we must first see that we have obtained the three sacraments which allow us fellowship with God. Then we need to seek a close relationship with fellow believers who will support us in our efforts to remain faithful. This would include our ministers and other bearers of blessing and those from whom we can learn God's words.

Finally, **no matter what the trap Satan uses to hold us in captivity, we must continuously pray, ask for forgiveness, cling to the altar of grace, and strive to overcome.** This means that because we love God, *truly* love Him and all He stands for, we hate our sin and we wish we did not commit our sins.

This hearts attitude assures us that God will be with us and that **we are weakening the hold which Satan may have on us.** This allows us to be forgiven. Whether or not we believe that our suffering will never end, we must understand that by clinging to the altar, we prove our faith and loyalty to God.

Our faith is dependent and supported by our understanding, knowledge and application of God's words and His plan of salvation. Our ability to sustain and enhance our faith and be found worthy is commensurate with our trust in God. Our ability to accept that which God allows into our life often is the measure of our trust in Him. When we believe that everything is under God's control and can be worked to the benefit of our soul, we lose most of our fear and find peace even in adversity.

The end times will be incredibly difficult because just before Christ comes, as all the signs predicted by scripture unfold, Satan sees and recognizes them and fights harder. He does not want to lose his freedom and seeks to break our faith so God does not attain that number of souls He longs for.

Bullet Points

- God knows that Satan becomes more desperate and dangerous as the end times wind down.

- God understand what we must fight and is willing to forgive us.

- Clinging to the altar despite our sins will bring God's blessing.

- Satan's plan is to bring so much evil just before Christ returns that even the elect could fall.

- God will not intervene during these days thus our trust in Him will be truly tested.

Supporting Scripture

- Matthew 12:31,
- Matthew 12:35-36,
- Mark 3:29,
- John 13:44-45.
- Acts 21:28,
- Revelation 6:5-6,
- Revelation 7:13-14
- Revelation 7:16,
- Revelation 2:9

Clinging to the altar loosens Satan's hold

Photography by Matthew Burniston

Chapter Eight

WHAT IS GOD'S PLAN FOR ME?

It is not too late for any individual to seek God even if they never did before and even if they currently wallow in sin. It is not too late to learn God's words. And, it is not too late for us to share our faith and what we know about our Heavenly Father with others even if we are scorned for doing so.

All who would like to learn of God can attend or hold Bible study groups where one studies scripture and Satan's work as it is described in scripture. We can include our children and invite ministers to our home where discussions about hope and forgiveness and what scripture tells us can take place. We can **have fellowship with those who believe or seek to believe as we do and who support our desire to understand and to share the wisdom of scripture.** We can help one another deal with the scorn many, even family members, may express about our faith and our hope, and pray together and uplift one another. We can continue in our effort to learn what scripture says so we can answer questions, make godly decisions and bring effective testimony to others.

As we begin to understand God's plan, our lives change, our children learn, and we become a testimony to those with whom we come in contact. This strengthens our effectiveness when we work to gather, teach and support those God wants for the Bride of Christ. We can explain what is currently happening in the world and hold it up as a sign of the end times when we must stay watchful, heed God's warnings, and discuss how many of these occurrences are the fulfillment of biblical prophecy. We can read where scripture teaches that Satan also knows that Christ's return is imminent and has sent wolves among us to devour those who do not understand, those who are weak in faith and those who teeter on the edge of complacency. We can read the biblical story of the ten virgins which warns that only five out of ten of God's children will be ready when Christ returns and thus we must not become complacent but **keep on striving even if we tire, become discouraged, are afraid, or fail.**

It is through scripture that we learn that only half of those who consider themselves faithful will have prepared themselves well enough to stand firm in their faith by having prepared themselves properly. (Matthew 25: 1-12) We can also read in Matthew 24:40-42, that only half of those who fully *expect* to be found worthy *will* be found worthy. These verses tell us that of two working in a field *together*, only one will be taken and the other left behind, and that of two lying in a bed *together,* one will be taken and the other left behind. These verses, and many others, clearly provide us with a warning. They do *not* address both believers and non-believers, but *all believers*.

Further, scripture explains that God's children will find themselves in great travail before the return of Christ. During this time of travail, each of us will struggle. We cannot do the work of our soul salvation for someone else, nor will it be easy to do while we are in great travail. While we can attempt to help one another, each of us must be determined to bring effective testimony and encouragement to one another, but can only do so if our hearts know how to love and what scripture teaches us.

To truly love one another, we must learn *how* to express our love.... to God and to others.....and how He wants us to reach out to one another. *We* need to learn how to overcome to be the Bride God wants for His Son, and this must first be accomplished on ourselves before we can teach this to others. We must understand that we *will* go through hardship and must not lose our faith during this time even though many fellow-believers will. We must understand that **scripture does not allow for a lack of understanding.**

In fact, in Hosea 4:6 scripture tells us that God laments saying, *"My people will be lost for a lack of understanding."* God does not say after these words that He will get back to these people later, or will excuse them, or excuse their children, or that they have time to learn, but says clearly that they will be ***lost.***

Further, scripture warns that Satan can enter hearts, conquer peoples, divide families and cause people to harm people. Those who do not provide this instruction to their family and those they carry a responsibility for are termed in scripture as those who have heard but not heeded God's instruction. The end times in which we now live are the last call to prepare ourselves and learn of God. It is our last opportunity to come into His presence, seek His love and protection, and have our sins forgiven. It is the time to build our trust and to understand that we will be tested and required to stand firm in great tribulation.

Grace is still offered today and provides the opportunity to correct our path and move to those things which have everlasting value. Those who do not make this effort will be held accountable not only for themselves, but also **held accountable for those who they caused to stumble.** Malachi 2:8 warns, *"But ye are departed out of the way, ye have caused many to stumble...."* Matthew 18:6 warns, *"But whoso shall offend one o f these little ones which believe in me; it were better for him that a millstone were hanged about his neck, and that he were drowned....."*

These verses tell us that we must share what we know with others so we are not the cause of their failure. Thus we need to continue as workers in the vineyard and must be an example of strength when travail envelopes the children of God. When we are strong and help those who are weak, when we are weak they will be our strength.

Acts 2:20 tells us, *"The sun shall be turned into darkness, and the moon into blood, before that great and notable day of the Lord come."* Acts 2:37 adds that *"Now when they heard this, they were pricked in their heart, and said unto Peter, and to the rest of the apostles, Men and brethren, what shall we do?"*

Scripture provides this answer in part when Peter replies in Acts 2:38-39, *"..... Repent, and be baptized every one of you in the name of Jesus Christ for the remission of sins, and ye shall receive the Holy Ghost. For the promise is unto you, and to your children, and to all that are afar off, even as many as the Lord our God shall call."* And then Acts 2:44 tells us, *"And all that believed were together, and had all things in common.* These verses, although stated so many years ago and for different circumstances, reflect the same instruction that is valid for today and was valid before.

God never changes. His words are constant and consistent. They teach, warn, encourage, promise and demonstrate a love so pure that we can learn from them what God hopes we will aspire to. Thus the answer to the question about what we should do as these times approach is to read scripture.

Discuss what it tells us. Prepare for the changes which will come. Prepare the family and the home for the times of tribulation. Prepare to help others who find themselves in need. Prepare to be a spiritual help to those whose fear overcomes their trust in God. Be steadfast. Be a role model. Be fearless in teaching God's words and in trusting God. Be sure to teach those for whom you are responsible, and prepare for those for whom you are or may become responsible.

Heed the warnings which may make life more bearable during the tribulation. Work to build the trust in God that will be required of you and those you love to help them stand firm in faith.... and despite any sin or failure, to cling to the Altar.

Scripture clearly tells us that Christians will be persecuted, that even the elect will be in great travail, and that many will lose their faith. It also warns us that even though we pray asking God to intervene, we will feel as if he is not intervening. By knowing this in advance and by prepare for these things we can better understand them when they come. We will know that despite what appears to be happening, God is still in control. Therefore, we will be able to withstand those days and God will bless us as He blessed Noah and Joseph for heeding His words.

Bullet Points

- Learning God's words is imperative

- Learning how to overcome what Satan is doing and will be doing is imperative.

- Helping others is a natural result of knowing the true love which God wants us to develop.

- Being aware that scripture tells us that we will be in great travail just before Christ comes will help us endure.

- Teaching our children what the end times will bring, will help them understand and protect their faith.

- Staying in fellowship with other children of God will provide the support required if one begins to falter.

Supporting Scripture

- Matthew 24:40-42,
- Matthew 25:1-12,
- Hosea 4:6,
- Malachi 2:8,
- Matthew 18:6,
- Acts 2:20,
- Acts 2:37,
- Acts 2:38-39,
- Acts 2:44

Photography by Matthew Burniston
Photo edit and verse overlay by Colette van Loggerenberg

Chapter Nine

WHAT IF I FAIL?

Scripture addresses the issue of fear and failure in many places throughout the Bible by reassuring us that God loves us, understands our concerns and looks after us. It is our failures which cause us to develop fear and guilt. However, **it is not our failures but the commitment and effort God sees us put forth which brings a blessing to us. It is what God sees in our heart and the striving that we exhibit which is what God looks for and loves....not our failures.** Matthew 6:14 tells us that we do not have to worry, Proverbs 1:33 tells us that we will be safe and secure, James 1:5 tells us we will be granted wisdom, and Proverbs 8:32 says "*Blessed are they that keep my ways*".

Additionally, scripture tells us in Hebrews 13:5 that God will never leave or forsake us, Exodus 33:22 tells us that God promises to cover us with His hand, John 14:27 tells us *"Let not your heart be troubled"*. **Isaiah 42:6 says, *"I will hold thine hand…"*, and Jeremiah 33:5 says *"Call to me and I will answer you"*.**

It is fascinating to find that in Psalm 46:1 David prayed, "*God is our refuge and strength, a very present help in trouble. Therefore we will not fear, though the earth be removed and though the mountains be carried into the midst of the sea.*" This verse seems directly related to the warning in Revelation 6:14 which says *".....and every mountain and island moved out of their places."*

These are special words for those who strive to know God and who seek His counsel.
As we study scripture and find one area of scripture supporting other areas and all providing the wisdom which God inspired in those who wrote the Bible, we can recognize its power and truth, tie them together, and absorb its validity and its miracle.

Nevertheless Satan tries to block this understanding and block our insight into scripture because knowing God's words helps us recognize Satan and strengthen our trust in God. He knows that if we falter, others may also falter. He knows that his time is limited if God finds that number of souls which scripture tells us He seeks.

Few of us think about the enormous power which belongs to Satan or how vulnerable we are to his whims. His power is far more immense than we can actually fathom and his hatred for the children of God drives him to do everything he can to break our faith. He realizes however, that if we were to recognize him and his work, we may scurry into the protective arms of our Heavenly Father. Thus, he is incredibly subtle in his attacks.

The natural instinct of fear which emanates from our Adam-like nature is an excellent weapon for him to use against us. Satan uses our fear to break our faith. He chooses this weapon because it allows him to work behind the scenes and in a manner which we may not notice yet which may cause us to slip ever so slightly toward a goal he has set with great patience and care. He does not want us to understand who he is, what he does, or why he does it.

Satan wants us to fear that there is no help and that we may falter under our burdens. He wants us to lose trust in God and believe that there is no help for us. Satan wants us to distrust *everything* scripture tells us. He knows that we would not strive to overcome if we did not trust God or those who reach out to help us. He wants us to distrust the importance of seeking forgiveness.

Satan is always working against us and against God's plan of salvation. He is always putting forth a huge effort to prevent or slow the work of our Heavenly Father. He does this by tweaking biblical truths and perverting them into a false doctrine or a false belief which works insidiously to place a wedge between God and His children. Once a small perversion is accepted by the human mind, it is easily exploited by Satan, and easily grows into a cancer which spreads and destroys man's trust in God or causes contention between God's children.

Scripture teaches us to speak sound doctrine (Titus 2:1), and to prove what we say and hear (Malachi 3:10, Romans 12:2, and 1 Thessalonians 5:21) by learning what God tells us in scripture. We must be especially careful when our troubles envelop us because scripture warns us that **Satan walks across**

the earth as a roaring lion seeking to devour us (1 Peter 5:8).

It is through our troubles that Satan seeks to destroy our faith, and thus prolong his freedom. We must take his power and desire very seriously. We must learn about Satan and use the wisdom we acquire to quell our fear and recognize from whence it comes. Our failures are used by Satan to discourage us.

It is during our times of tribulation when Satan exercises his greatest power. His desire is to cause us to wonder where God is, where righteousness is, and when God will stop the devastating harm we endure or witness. He wants us to believe that perhaps, because God does not step in to fix these ills, that there may be no God after all. He wants us to wonder why we cannot overcome those things we long to overcome. He wants us to feel unworthy and give up!

It is through these means that our faith and patience will be tested, thus our knowledge of what and why we must endure heartache and the faith we can develop during those times becomes hard to grasp. Yet, while we still have the opportunity to do so, is of utmost importance that we stand firm and do not allow failure to interfere with our faith. It will be too late to begin this exercise after we have been taken from the altar of grace.... or after the altar of grace is removed from earth.

But if we stay faithful, cling to the altar despite our failures, we will be those whom God can help and forgive and perhaps those who others turn to for advice. If we retain our faith through all circumstances we will be the teachers and strengtheners.

But to do so, we have to learn before it is too late. We have to strengthen our own faith to endure all things including the end times and our personal failures. The guilt and fear which Satan brings to us takes many paths and Satan uses them all. If one path fails, he finds another and it is only through prayer and our attachment to the altar that we can find the help we require.

We usually experience fear when we witness blatant evil or a threat to our well-being. But as we mentioned, Satan is subtle. He knows that we can also be immobilized by a minor fear such as someone who mocks our interpretation of scripture, or sneers at our concerns, or disapproves of our testimony or our striving, or those who claim they need no further preparation. Fear can come in the guise of worrying whether or not we remain "friends" with our children when we rebuke the actions which are displeasing to God.

However, we need to overcome these fears by exercising our trust in God. Therefore, it is to our advantage to begin to exercise the muscle of faith *now* and do so by initiating small moves into those areas which may make us uncomfortable yet we know to be right place to venture. As we experience success we grow in trust that God will support us and turn uncomfortable situations into triumphs as we stand firm for our Christian values. **The only real failure is to give up and leave the altar of grace.**

Prayer is the best way to begin such an effort. We can come to God in earnest, telling Him in prayer that we *are* afraid, that we *do* lack courage; that we *fear* alienating others, yet we believe that God wants us to speak up. Nevertheless, **God tells us that His strength is made manifest through our weakness.** Thus, we can ask God to help us and direct our path and open a conversation where we can make the effort we wish to make. This type of intimate conversation with God brings us closer to Him and also opens the way for God to prove Himself as standing beside us, caring for us and helping us whether or not we sometimes fail. God loves to do this for us.

In fact, Malachi 3:10 tells us, *".....and prove me now herewith, saith the Lord of hosts, if I will not open you the windows of heaven, and pour you out a blessing, that there shall not be room enough to receive it."*

Bullet Points

- The only real failure is to give up
- Satan wants to keep us away from the altar of grace.
- God recognizes and rewards a striving heart.
- Satan works to break our faith and striving.
- God looks at our sincerity rather than our failures
- Receiving Holy Communion worthily breaks Satan's past hold on us

Supporting Scripture

- Malachi 3:10,
- Hebrews 13:5,
- Jeremiah 33:5.
- Revelation 6:14,
- Psalm 46:1,
- Isaiah 42:6,
- John 14:27,
- Exodus 33:22,
- Proverbs 8:32,
- Proverbs 1:33,
- Matthew 6:14,
- James 1:5

Photography and verse overlay by
Colette van Loggerenberg

Chapter Ten

HOW CAN OTHERS HELP?

Counsel requires compassion and an understanding of human nature. It requires us to be aware that we often feel guilty when we cannot overcome the pain, fear and failure which life's circumstances can create. Because we are children of God, we want to control these emotions through our trust in God. Thus, living with negative emotions can make us feel guilty and unworthy of God's help and even wonder if we lack sufficient faith. It helps if we understand that we are born with a survival mechanism which uses pain and fear to protect us from harm.

Just as we fight Satan more wisely when we understand his nature and why and how he seeks to harm us, and we utilize the power of prayer because we know what God can do, we can also fight our human nature when we understand how it works. By learning about our natural emotional make-up we can assess what is happening to us and why, and find the resources with which to fight.

Our human nature is built into our psyche, is an innate need to protect and survive and uses emotion to warn us of danger or draw us to happiness. Even Christ felt fear and fought this part of His human nature before He could submit to the will of His Father. As children of God we know that with every difficult circumstance we overcome we grow stronger spiritually and emotionally. Understanding what we feel and why, and how to move from pain to trust and acceptance, changes the way we react to circumstances and makes them easier to bear. Learning how to deal with our human nature helps us become successful in our spiritual life. Both have to be understood for them to grow stronger.

Grief is a debilitating emotion and is the result of loss; even a perceived loss. It can be triggered by the death of a child, spouse or parent; the end of a romance or marriage; the loss of a home, a job, our savings; the loss of one's health or the health of a loved one; or anything else that we believe is of great importance to us. A study of the effects of grief was conducted by a Swiss-born American psychiatrist named Elisabeth Kubler- Ross. During her study she discovered that the reactions to grief included denial, anger, bargaining, depression and acceptance and that most of us must experience all of these conditions before we can heal. She determined that when we sense a potential loss, our human nature place us into a state of denial where we unconsciously ignore or deny the first signs of a problem. Our psyche decides that everything will work out and what we feel will somehow be resolved and allows us to remain in denial until reality is unavoidable. Others move through denial and into the next stage more quickly.

The second stage of grief is anger. Anger can be directed inward, toward the circumstance, toward the person we believe caused the loss, or even toward those who counsel us. Satan is delighted to have us remain in this stage of grief and even more delighted if we blame God and then live with guilt. But God knows that we battle not only Satan, but the very nature with which we were born. He wants to help us recognize these truths and understand why we feel as we do and how we can move through and away from those feelings. He wants to turn our loss into a victory.

Once we move past anger, we move into the stage of bargaining. We bargain with whomever we believe can change our circumstance, including God. We promise to do better, to work harder, to make up for every wrong thought or action if only the circumstance would be removed. As children of God we hope that by going to church more often, praying more often, tithing more and working harder in the vineyard, we will garner the favor of God who may then remove our cross.

When these three stages fail to help us, we may move back and forth between them once again or fall into the fourth stage of grief which is depression. Depression creates great internal sorrow, and is the result of an inner decision that the pain is too difficult to fight. Depression destroys our hope for future joy. But once this stage is successfully navigated, we move into the healing stage of acceptance where the energy for everyday tasks returns and we accept our loss. When we understand our human nature, we move through the stages of grief more quickly. When those who counsel us also understand that these stages of emotion are a natural part of the make-up of mankind, they counsel with greater compassion and effectiveness.

This understanding allows us to recognize the stages of grief and why the pain and fear is not easily and immediately overcome. It also prevents us from innocently heaping guilt on an already battered soul which believes that if they continue to experience pain and fear, they are not trusting God.

While the soul and the spiritual make-up of that person knows this to be true, the pain to their physical make-up is too great for them to utilize this information. But with compassion, patience and an explanation of what is happening internally and why, the soul can move away from the pain, guilt and isolation, and into the love, compassion and advice of their faith…. and heal. The end result is a stronger child of God and a stronger, more compassionate counselor. This understanding creates a bond between the two, and souls able to reach out with that same understanding to help someone else. Satan does not want us to understand human nature and wants us to feel guilt and give up trying. He wants us to feel that because we continue to experience pain and fear, and even anger, we are not a true child of God.

But God wants us to know that our human nature is a part of us and with His help we can move through these stages quickly and overcome its negative effects. Satan wants to block our understanding, while God wants to create a blessing from it. With God's help, a child of God does not have to bow before their human nature, but can begin to understand its process and use the power of their faith and the love and support of their bearers of blessing to overcome it.

It is difficult to live through heartbreaking circumstances especially when it seems that God does not hear nor answer our prayers. When difficulties continue with no end in sight we can become discouraged and perhaps question our faith, or question our worthiness to have our prayers heard. We may even wonder what we did wrong to deserve what has befallen us. These are normal reactions, but they are not godly; they come from Satan and must be fought. Satan wants us discouraged by heartache and wants us to blame God, feel unworthy of His help, and question His lack of intervention. When Satan succeeded in causing Adam and Eve to sin and thereby opened the door to sin, we were subject to battle not only our own sin, but the inherited sin which scripture later defines as a type of "generational" sin which is visited upon the third and fourth generations.

This tells us that the weaknesses of our forefathers may have transferred to us and may be the source of addictions and tendencies that are difficult to fight. But, God factored this into His plan of salvation and provided us with a way to overcome and offers His comforting presence during our struggle. Our Heavenly Father, omnipotent and omnipresent, clearly tells us in Romans 8:28, *"And we know that all things work together for good to them that love God, to them who are called according to his purpose."*

There is a reason why we must live through heartache. When we understand why God allows our struggles they are easier to bear and the blessing we can derive from the experience may become evident more quickly. Our job is to believe that a blessing does come from our experience. And to believe that good comes from what transpires in our heart as we go through our difficult circumstances. When we know what scripture tells us about this phenomena we can place our faith in God's help and wisdom.

Scripture tells us that God does not bring our heartache, but that Satan does, and that God in His perfect righteousness must allow it. However, just as God went with Shadrach, Meshach and Abed-nego into the furnace (Daniel 3:20), and with Daniel into the den of lions (Daniel 6:6), and with David when he faced Goliath (1 Samuel 17:49), He goes with us. He turns our heartache into a blessing in a way that we do not understand but which we later learn has established our loyalty to God and strengthens us in the process. But when we are not aware that it is Satan who brings our heartache and God creates a blessing from it, our heartache is more difficult to bear, and the blessing harder to recognize.

The Biblical account of Sodom and Gomorra teaches us God's compassion as we read that He agreed to Abraham's plea (Genesis 18:32) to save Lot and his family from the destruction of the city. We learn of His patience when Jonah ran from God (Jonah 1:3), we understand His gentleness through the beatitudes Christ spoke (Matthew 5:3-11), we see his longsuffering in all His references to us as children rather than adults, and we see His love throughout the beauty of the creation that He made just for us. When we have an intimate relationship with our Heavenly Father, His words touch a chord in our heart that allows us to internalize His loving, gentle nature.

With these facts in our heart and mind we trust God more easily and are more likely to muster our strength to wait patiently for our circumstances to change. We can dismiss our fear, anxiety, and doubt, and most importantly, thank God for our circumstances because we know that they bring valuable changes to our heart to create in us one who can become a part of the Bride of Christ. Fellowship with other believers can help us. If we share our worries and triumphs with one another and bear one another's burdens we will uplift one another in times of sorrow. We can pray for one another, remind one another of the various verses in scripture that may pertain to our circumstance, bask in the promise that God never leaves us, and love, forgive and encourage one another.

God loves us. He teaches us through the difficulties Satan brings into our lives. He works miracles through what we go through and is pleased when we use our experiences to help others move through their difficulties. He wants us to grow from children to the Bride of Christ which can only be accomplished if we develop in love and understanding, compassion and strength. As Christians, we must remember that if we never felt pain, we would not know that God is our healer. If we never had to pray we would not know that He delivers us from our difficulties.

If we never felt sadness, we would not feel His comfort. If we never had a trial to go through, we could never call ourselves overcomers. If we were never in trouble, how would we know that God always comes to our rescue? If we never suffered, how would we understand the suffering of others, or what Christ suffered on the cross? And if we were never broken, how would we learn that God can make us whole? If our life was perfect, we might not have the opportunity to know God and recognize how much we need Him and how much He does for us.

We should marvel at how profound it is that God turns evil into good so that all things work for the good of those who love the Lord. And, we should marvel at how much this can comfort us as we go through our trials and tribulations. We also have the incredible promise of Revelation 2:10: *"Fear none of those things which thou shalt suffer...."* And Revelation 21:4: *"And God shall wipe away all tears from their eyes; and there shall be no more death, neither sorrow, nor crying, neither shall there be any more pain...."*

For some, God's compassion provides them with an excuse to continue to sin and to continue in their complacency. It does not because God can read the private recesses of every heart. Further, even if one believes that our Heavenly Father has placed into the physics of this world every opportunity and every manner of invitation and instruction for us to learn of Him and follow Him, they should not believe that there is plenty of time left to make that choice. There is not. We must make the choice between good and evil on our own and soon. The bottom line is that we have but one of two choices to make and the one must be made right away. To serve evil can be a choice or can be the result of no choice or a choice not to follow God. To serve God is a single choice and one that then requires we demonstrate our commitment to that choice.

Our Heavenly Father is so perfectly righteous that as He draws us, He is required to work under His own rules of righteousness, which prevents Him from forcing us to bow our hearts and knees and follow. Thus, if we choose not to follow or when we turn away, He does not force us. When we make a choice that results in our not following God, He must let us go even if He plans to try again another day. However, the longer we resist the more hardened our heart becomes and the stronger the hold Satan has on us becomes.

Satan knows when we come close to making a commitment to God and uses his power to disrupt that commitment. As stated previously, Satan will remain free until God reaches the number He longs for. The more souls Satan can take away from a decision to follow God, the longer he believes that he can remain unfettered to prolong his war. Satan knows the rules under which God has chosen to labor in His effort to draw us to Him and therefore works hard to cause man to lose his faith or never even make a covenant with God.

As we gain an understanding of this process we can begin to understand that the war between God and Satan has become a war over us. It is a quest to claim the soul of man either for good or for evil. This is the "spiritual warfare" that takes place every day here on earth. It will continue until Christ returns. Those not taken by Christ at the First Resurrection will face the full wrath of Satan until Satan is bound. Because Satan succeeded in causing them to choose not to follow God and to choose to follow Satan they will never find grace but will be judged and become either what scripture calls a “goat” to spend eternity with Satan, or become what scripture calls a “ lamb”, which can enter heaven, but ***not*** abide in the City of God.

Because our Heavenly Father wants to fill His kingdom with souls who will truly love Him and His Son, and also love one another, we must voluntarily practice how to truly love, trust, and exhibit loyalty. God’s love provides that until Christ returns it is not too late to make these adjustments to our lives. God offers grace and the forgiveness of our sins so we can become a part of His future community.

But Satan has the ability to blind the minds of men and he has exercised that ability so that many cannot see the truth of scripture.

God understands that we must live under the attacks of Satan. He knows that life’s pressures may keep us from studying scripture. Yet He willingly provides us with a myriad of opportunities to learn.

Because God is a righteous God, and offers every soul what they require both naturally and spiritually, we cannot excuse our failure by saying that we didn't know or could not find a way.

Satan knows God's plan too and he fully understands that when this plan is completed and Christ returns, Satan will be thrown into hell. To forestall his fate Satan must destroy our trust in God and our desire to do His will. God, knowing what Satan will do, has provided us with warnings and protection to avoid the trap Satan will lay for us as he fights vehemently for his continued freedom.

God has allotted a certain amount of time for His children to be made ready which only he knows. Matthew 24:36 tells us, *"But of that day and hour knoweth no man, no, not the angels oh heaven, but my Father only."* Acts 1:7 tells us, *"And he said unto them, It is not for you to know the times or the seasons, which the Father hath put in his own power."*

But when that time does arrive, Christ will return to earth for the First Resurrection to take to heaven both those from eternity who have obtained forgiveness and those alive who are faithful. (James 1:18; 1 John 5:4; Revelation 2:7, 11, 26; Revelation 3:5, 12, 21, Revelation 12:5 and 11; Revelation 21:7) When they are gone, grace will also be gone, and the completion of the great tribulation and destruction will begin where one third of all those remaining on the earth will die. (Daniel 12:1-2; Matthew 24:21-22; Thessalonians 2:1-4; 2 Timothy 3:1-9)

Our Heavenly Father also arranges that even the unbeliever will hear or read this warning at some point in their lifetime. If this is not possible then that word will be brought to them in eternity so that everyone will have the opportunity to know what God offers and can accept or decline, work, or remain complacent. It is a personal decision to seek God and to work toward building an intimate relationship with him…. or not.

God provides many opportunities to learn of Him and provides many avenues to learn which accommodates our lifestyles. Further, He tells us that if we ask for His help He will give it, and if we seek, He guarantees that we will find what we seek. However, when those doors are opened to us, we will be held responsible if God knocked on our hearts-door and we closed that door to Him.

We will also be held responsible for those for whom we were given the responsibility to teach and did not. To ignore these things can result in an eternity in hell in a soul that never dies. God calls us, He loves us, He wants to forgive us, and help us, and He longs to spend all eternity with us if we simply allow Him into our hearts and learn of Him. The tribulations of the end times will be very difficult, but God has given us a way to make it a little less difficult physically, spiritually and emotionally. Whether or not we take that advice and use it is up to us.

Bullet Points

- Heartache comes from Satan, not from God.
- We realize that we need God when we endure difficult circumstances.
- God uses our heartache to mold us into His children.
- We learn compassion for others when we experience our own heartache.
- Our suffering is easier to bear when we know why it is occurring.
- Faith increases when we see God helping us through our difficulties.
- Satan flees when we do not lose our hope or our trust in God.
- We will be held responsible if we fail to teach our children about God's words in scripture and His plan of salvation.
- God forgives our failures if we strive to overcome them.

Supporting Scripture

- James 1:18,
- John 5:4,
- Revelation 2:7,
- Revelation 2:11
- Revelation 2:26,
- Revelation 3:5,
- Revelation 3:12,
- Revelation 3:21,
- Revelation 12:5,
- Revelation 12:11,
- Revelation 21:7,
- Daniel 12:1-2,
- Matthew 24:21-22,
- Thessalonians 2:1-4,
- 2 Timothy 3:1-9,
- Matthew 24:6,
- Revelation 2:10,
- Revelation 24:4,
- Matthew 5:3-11,
- Romans 8:28,
- Daniel 3:20,
- Daniel 6:6,
- 1 Samuel 17:49,
- Genesis 18:32,
- Jonah 1:3

"And God shall wipe away
all tears from their eyes;
and there shall be no more death,
neither sorrow, nor crying,
neither shall there be any more pain. . . ."

Revelation 21:4

Photography by Colette van Loggerenberg

Bibliography

New Apostolic Church. *The Holy Bible* (King James Version). Canada: Thomas Nelson, Inc., 1972.

New Apostolic Church. *The Holy Bible* (New King James Version). North America: Thomas Nelson Publishers, 1994.

Strong, James. *Strong's Exhaustive Concordance of the Bible.* Abington, Nashville, 1890.

New Revised Standard Version of the Apocrypha, Oxford University Press, Inc., 1991

About The Author

Helen Gumienny Glowacki is an interior designer, writer, teacher, and motivational speaker. She was the host, writer, and producer of the television series *The Contemporary Woman*, broadcast by UA-Columbia Cablevision, which addressed interior design and the health, relationship, parenting, and life issues of interest to women.

Helen also co-hosted a number of twenty-four-hour telethons featuring celebrity guests to raise funds for various community projects and was a guest co-host for a cable television game show.

Helen's writing credentials include an extensive background as a freelance feature writer and a staff writer for four newspapers; author of newsletter articles; developer of marketing manuals, most notably for the INOVA Hospital System; and designer and editor of a newsletter for the Martin/St. Lucie Chapter of the United States Amateur Ballroom Dancers Association.

A graduate of William Paterson University, Helen received her Bachelor of Arts degree in communications, magna cum laude. Helen also has an associate of science degree with honors and is a registered nurse. She has served on the boards of directors for two associations and taught interior design for adult school programs. Some of her larger design projects include Avon Headquarters in Morton Grove, Illinois, and Chilton Hospital in Pequannock, New Jersey and was listed in *Who's Who of American Women* and *Who's Who of Women Executives* in 1992.

As a popular speaker at ease with an audience, Helen addresses aspects of interior design and addresses the work of God and His word through scripture. Her venues have included women's groups, church groups, community service and religious organizations, high schools and colleges, libraries, cruise ships, and large adult—and assisted-living condominium complexes.

Helen appeared as a guest on a radio show and performed dance routines for theater groups, television, army camps, and veteran's hospitals. She held the title Mrs. Packanack Lake for five years and has received a number of community service awards.

Helen has donated her "*Grandmother Series*" novels, her "*Why God Why Series*" and other non-fiction books to cancer centers, drug and alcohol rehabilitation centers, prisons and mission schools, most notably to *The Henwood Foundation* in Zambia, Africa to bring testimony. She also posts articles on her Facebook wall which address our relationship with God,

Helens greatest joys are her husband, two children, and four grandchildren, and her New Apostolic Church activities. She and her husband enjoy ballroom dancing and have performed for various charitable functions. Her heart's desire is to help others find the love and comforting presence of God through her writing.

****

To learn more about Helen's novels and her non-fiction books, visit her website at www.helenglowacki.com.

To become a distributor or to purchase in quantity for a fund raising project or to provide testimony, please send an email to helen@helenglowacki.com.

Helen's readers can also visit the author on Face Book at http://www.facebook.com/pages/The-Grandmother-Series/155300907853909?ref=ts.

"And the Spirit,

and the bride say,

Come.

And let him that heareth

say, Come,

and let him that is

athirst come.

And whosoever will,

let him take the

water of life freely."

Revelation 22:17

Excerpt from

Overcoming Depression: HOW TO BE HAPPY

Those who see the silver lining in every circumstance and find their cup half full rather than half empty are those who seem to rise effortlessly above even the most difficult circumstances. If such an attitude were for sale, we would purchase as much as we could afford!

Since all of us face problems which make our lives difficult it is natural to wonder how others seem to bear their circumstances with little fear. What makes ones person happy and another saddened by similar events? Why is it that some become discouraged, frightened, impatient and heartbroken, when life throws us a curve and others take it in stride? Why do some fall into depression and others do not? And how can we become more like those who bear their burdens with nobility?

The answer lies in understanding our Adam-like nature and learning why scripture tells us to shed that nature to develop a Christ-like nature. Understanding why the Adam-like nature causes us to react as we do helps us immensely in understanding how to overcome it.

God lovingly provides us, through scripture, with everything we need to know so we can understand our circumstances and learn how to be an overcomer. He lays everything out to help us understand why we fall prey to those circumstances which Satan can use against us. But once we learn God's words, understand how sin and the Adam-like nature keep us bound, we can emerge victorious. We begin to understand what is offered and how to use what is offered and we can then begin to overcome our stumbling and be found worthy.

Once again, Helen Glowacki has created a self-help book which is inspiring as it uncovers incredible information and provides a wonderful explanation of the many faces of sadness. Her readers have said that they have had an “aha” moment from which they can make positive changes to their lives.

This addition to Helen’s non-fiction books helps us understand how we can be happy despite what we must endure.

Novels

By Helen Glowacki (Book Size 6 x 9)

When God Broke Grandma's Heart: (208 pages) Rising from sorrow to become a beacon of faith Grandma struggles in an abusive marriage until God moves her from unequally yoked and broken to the healing of His love and forgiveness. Her granddaughter Sarah learns where to find answers to her problems and carries that legacy to those she loves. **Paperback: ISBN 978-1-9847-2110-8**

When God Took Grandma Home: (268 pages) About the heartache of drug addiction, of the enemy who destroys children through drugs, why God allows righteous anger, why we should pray for those in eternity and a description an incredible experience of faith for Matt and Sarah about why God allowed such heartache to occur.
Paperback: ISBN 978-1-9847-2111-5

When Grandma Chased the Spirits: (216 Pages) The magnetism of idolatry, it's invisible power, and the heartache of bearing a child out of wedlock brings debilitating panic attacks to Mary and affects her husband Kevin. When Matt and Sarah tell them about their faith, God engineers a miracle to solve what that they thought impossible to resolve. **Paperback: ISBN 978-1-0847-2112-2**

The Granddaughter and the Monkey Swing: (292 pages) A wedding, a broken engagement, renóvating and decorating a home through Divine Proportion, the truth about Halloween, and the gift of role models create a tender story of friendship. Helping through the planning and problems of a wedding culminates in the unveiling of a secret. **Paperback: ISBN 978-1-9847-211309**

Grandma's Little Book of Poetry: The Story of God's Plan of Salvation: (285 pages) This beautiful whimsical story for all ages, begins when Sarah finds a manuscript in Grandma's desk and recognizes the story Grandma read to her and Josh and Caleb when they were children. Angels watch the inhabitants below them struggle to find God. **Paperback: ISBN 978-1-9847-2114-6**

Abiding Faith, Hidden Treasure: (270 pages) Serving in Iraq, Jim loses his faith to see a loving God allow so much heartache. Barbara invites him to dinner where Grandma shows him why creation and evolution co-exist and God's enemy creates the

injustices Jim blames on God. Letters from the grave bring an incredible experience of faith.
Paperback: ISBN 978-1-9847-2115-3

And Then They Asked God: (295 Pages) When Rebecca and Jayden arrive at their college campus they are overwhelmed by betrayal. Losing the values Rebecca once cherished fills her with guilt so monumental that she cannot forgive herself. Jayden tries to help Rebecca but is framed for something he did not do. But Chaldeth, the evil angel, is defeated when God's grace allows the truth to surface and also brings about Rebecca's recovery.
Paperback: ISBN 978-1-9847-2116-0

Non-Fiction Books

by Helen Glowacki (Book size: 5 ½ x 8 ½)

Politically Incorrect: The Get Some Gumption Handbook when Enough is Enough: (408 pages) Fifty timely and controversial issues are examined under the politically correct approach along with a description of what scripture says is the approach that God wants His children to take. **Paperback: ISBN 978-1-4507-9074-1**

Overcoming Depression: How To Be Happy: (248 pages) We all face heartache, and all feel sad from time to time. But depression comes from a satanic attack that robs us of hope and our relationship with God. Thus our Heavenly Father tells us through scripture how we can tap into His blessing and find joy even in tribulation.
Paperback: ISBN 978-1-4507-9077-2

What No One Tells You About Addictions: (216 pages) Discussing the merits of tough love, the selfish co-dependency of the enabler, what scripture tells us about spiritual warfare and invasion, and generational sin, make this book a must read. **Paperback: ISBN 978-1- 4507--9075-8**

The Why God Why Mini-Series

By Helen Glowacki (Book size: 5 ½ x 8 ½)

To What Purpose?: (126 pages) The first book of the *Why God Why* series is written to provide answers to questions about why we are here and what we need to learn. It is written in an easy to read and easy to understand manner and one you will want to share.
Paperback: ISBN 978-1-4507-7580-9

Why God, Why?: (126 pages) This second book in the *Why God Why* Series describes why we experience heartache, its purpose, and how to face it. It answers questions about God's plan for us and what we need to do to be found worthy.
Paperback: ISBN 978-1-4507-7581-6

Why Trust Scripture?: (126 pages) This third book in the *Why God, Why* Series addresses the challenges against scripture, who wrote the Bible, the importance of the sacraments, what role Satan plays, and how health and the Bible are related. **Paperback: ISBN 978-1-4507-7582-3**

What Should I Know about Life after Death and the Coming Tribulation?: (126 pages) What occurs following death, what will happen during the tribulation, and what the seven seals could mean to us are explained in this fourth book of the series. **Paperback: ISBN 978-1-4507-7583-0**

What Does God Want Me to do Right Now?: (126 pages) A concise explanation of what God asks of us, how we can live up to His expectations what is required to become a part of the Bride of Christ, and what God plans for the future with or without us. **Paperback: ISBN 978-1 4507-9076-5**

Do The Little Sins REALLY Count?: (126 pages) Most of us believe that the little sins we commit each day are not important on the grander scale, but what does scripture tell us? And interesting look at the Bride of Christ. **Paperback: ISBN 978-9847-2117-7**

Book Reviews

Rev. Richard C. Freund, President, New Apostolic Church USA, Sea Cliff, New York: Magnificent writer, a story that makes the reader become emotionally involved, a joy to read, strong Christian values. ***"When God Broke Grandma's Heart",*** best seller quality.

Rev. Fred Krueger, (Ret.) Lutheran Minister 12 yrs and Clinical Social Worker 26 yrs, Dallas, Texas: "Inspiring, grabs the heart, author headed to the bestseller list, a pleasure to read, masterful. ***"When God Took Grandma Home"*** filled with insight into God's plan!

Rev. Richard C. Freund, President, New Apostolic Church USA, Sea Cliff, New York: ***"When God Took Grandma Home"*** "Delights, brings comfort to those who grieve. Inspires, gives insight into the after-life, masterful portrayal.

Priest Derryck Beukes, Montana-De Aar Congregation, Northern Cape, South Africa: Dear Helen, I personally often use your articles in my soul care visits, especially where youth are involved. I can assure you that your articles made a difference to my way of thinking, and I am busy encouraging fellow priests to read your works, as they are so factual and insightful! Thank you for your hard work. II thank God for you, and the wisdom He gave you! Please continue with the excellent work.

Deacon Shadreck Wilima, Overspill Congregation, Ndola, Zambia: Your articles prompt realistic examples which New Apostolic Christians need for their everyday living.

Youth Chairperson, Sunday School teacher, Mulenga Ernest, Lusaka Central Congregation, Lusaka, Zambia: Through your writing I am constantly reminded of what to be aware of. I pray that God keeps you in the hollow of His hand, guards you and guides you to reach your brethren as you do me. Thanks for caring for the souls of many.

Priest Aurelio Cerullo, Atripalda Congregation, Campania, Southern Italy: Your books and articles, and even your social networking are a means to bring brothers and sisters the words of our faith and to touch the hearts of those who do not know our faith. Our goal can still be found through the grace of the apostolate and in this sense, the word's from 1 Corinthians 15:58 assumes an important meaning: *"Therefore, my beloved brethren, be steadfast, immovable, always abounding in the work of the Lord, Knowing That your labor is not in vain in the Lord".* Now that I am a minister of God for about a year I too am grateful to our beloved Father in Heaven for having opened the eyes of my soul, for having removed the plugs from my ears of my heart to hear and listen to His will in connection and communion with those who precede us, guided by the light of the Holy Spirit. God's work always evolves and adapts to the times and even via computers, cell phones and smart phones. I Thank God for having been able to know you, you're a very valuable pearl. God bless you richly.

NOTE: The articles which are referred to in the above listed reviews are excerpts from Helen Glowacki's non-fiction books. Not shown are reviews by the ministers who oversee *The Henwood Foundation*'s New Apostolic Mission Schools in Zambia who review all reading materials prior to distribution.

Priest Andrew Muliokela, Alexandria Virginia congregation: ***The Granddaughter and the Monkey Swing*** and this series of books is awesome! A journey unlike another, read a great novel, learn about confidence, love and support but also learning

Bible verses at the same time! Helen Glowacki teaches through her books and I recommend them 100%. You'll enjoy the journey!

Priest Kevin Speranza, Palm Beach Gardens Congregation, Florida: ***And Then They Asked God*** so happy I read this, weaves and documents biblical precepts, addresses political correctness, moral & political corruption, biased teaching, the insidious growth of socialism renamed progressivism, self-importance, guilt and its debilitating power. WELL DONE! Identifies danger, artfully shows Biblically how to address them.

Frederick Rothe, Retired NAC Minister, Fort Pierce, Florida: Retired minister spending 48 years serving God another 30 in the congregation. These books contain an accurate account of what God wants of us, why we suffer. The application of scripture and the people in the stories stand for the principles God wants in all of us.

Patricia Robinson, wife of a Ret. Rector, Indiana 5 star rating: ***When God Broke Grandma's Heart***: WONDERFUL INSPIRATIONAL NOVEL, enjoyed this book, well written, Bible references , how to achieve peace of mind and soul .

Colette van Loggerenberg, wife of a Priest, Scottsville Congregation of Pietermaritzberg, South Africa: ***Grandma's Little Book of Poetry: The Story of God's Plan of Salvation:*** This has to be one of the BEST EVER books that I have read....If you ever get the chance to get one of Helen's novels...READ IT. It's like a fairytale but a TRUE fairytale.....Close your eyes and picture this: Grandma with her hair in a bun, glasses perched delicately on her nose, sitting delicately on her nose, sitting in a rocking chair with her grandchildren sitting on the floor with BIG eyes hanging onto her every word.....but with a twist!!!!! If you have doubts about PRAYERS...read this book. I LOVED IT...thank you Helen Glowacki in a rocking chair and her grandchildren sitting on the floor with BIG eyes hanging onto her every word.....but with a twist!!!!! If you have doubts about PRAYER...read this book. I LOVED IT...thank you!

Debbie Espeland, wife of a Rector, Palm Beach Gardens Congregation, Florida: 5 star rating: **When God Took Grandma Home** is so HEARTWARMING! This book touched my heart. It is both heartwarming and very spiritual.

Aletta Venter, wife of a Deacon, Scottsville Congregation, Pietermaritzburg, South Africa: ***"Grandma's Little Book of Poetry: The Story of God's Plan of Salvation".*** What a learning process for me. Oooh I just **love** the way the angels are telling the story, **very original!** When is mankind ever going to learn? The inhabitant's lesson was to learn of good and evil. And they failed miserably each time. The devil has his agenda, and the inhabitants are the target. They call upon God for help, the angels rejoiced. Great....!!!

Priest Luke Jansen, Sr. V. P., Medical Connections, Boca Raton, Florida: "To Ms. Glowacki, author of **The Grandma Series**: grateful for your books, refreshing to find a Christian author who sees the *difference* between religion and spirituality AND that the two can and should be used in the same sentence."

Aletta Venter, wife of a Deacon, Pietermaritzburg, South Africa: ***"Abiding Faith, Hidden Treasure"*** is the deepest and most rewarding novel I have ever read, touched my soul, made me cry, author's understanding of God's work is astounding, opens the mysteries

Katharina Leipp, Schopfheim, Germany: This is the first time I have ever heard of a female New Apostolic author and I am very impressed by your articles. I have sent your link to my Shepherd and German friends and would like you to consider advertising in our German *Our Family Magazine.*

Rosemarie Schaal, wife of a retired Evangelist, Palm City, Florida: ***Abiding Faith, Hidden Treasure:*** Reader develops empathy, feels emotion, hears a battle between scientific and spiritual knowledge. Skillful, detailed, brilliant, vivid, teaches nothing happens that is not planned by Him.

Claudine Visagie, South Africa: I'm trying to think of a way to introduce Helen's books and articles to others… especially to our youth. They are life changing!

Rabecca Mukuta Mukato, Lusaka, Zambia, Africa: Speaking on behalf of my Dad, District Elder Mulako, your articles are brilliant because they have changed me! Because of your articles my Dad has less headaches!

Edith Stier, 32 Years as the wife of a Minister, (Ret. Dist. Ev), Clifton, New Jersey: *The Grandma Series* helps those in need, inspirational, heartwarming, ends with a beautiful example of how God explains our pain, renews hope, shows us the way, creates miracles. I love this series.

Tammera Shelton, M.S. Psychology, Odenton, Maryland: I find "***When God Broke Grandma's Heart"*** inspirational, beautifully portrays need to let go of negative events and that despite injustice, no pain is for naught.

Robert W. Rothe, USMC 1970-1976, Nevada: 5 star rating: ***When God Broke Grandma's Heart:*** Outstanding writer, kept me riveted, an angel sent to help through trying days. Thank you for helping me find peace.

Frank Geores, from Port St. Lucie, Florida: "***When Grandma Chased The Spirits:*** beautiful spiritual experience, can see caring nature and loving heart of author, eloquently reveals her love for God and search for truth. Worthy of the Star of

Bethlehem rating. Thank you for sharing your magnificent gift.

Ben Lodwick, Avid Reader., from Brookfield, Wisconsin: Wow! An eye opener about God's plan of salvation, and why bad things happen to good people. Reminds me of Jim LaHaye and Jerry B. Jenkins "Left Behind Series". MUST READ!"

Dr. Walter Forman From North Palm Beach, Florida: ***Grandma's Little Book of Poetry: The Story of God's Plan of Salvation:*** a "wonderful book about success and failure in life. All Helen's novels are wonderful, a balm for the soul and an education to the seeker."

Susan Day, From Jupiter, Florida: ***Abiding Faith, Hidden Treasure*** : I hated to put it down, couldn't wait to pick it up, read all Helen's books, proves every point, shows what to do through God's words. I am 90 and Helen's books have helped me call on God.

Georgette Rothe, From Fort Piece, Florida: ***Abiding Faith, Hidden Treasure*** was more than I expected, like a Biblical course making you re-evaluate your beliefs, enjoyed the journey very much.

Fred D'Alauro, from Palm Beach Shores, Florida: Internet 5 star rating: **When God Took Grandma Home:** Remarkable! Inspirational and moving. A fascinating storyteller with a real message.

<u>Debra Forman, Chester, New York.</u> Internet 5 star rating: ***When God Broke Grandma's Heart***: Written from the heart, shares the strong beliefs that shelters us in times of need, courage captivates the reader. Thank you.

<u>Anonymous:</u> Internet 5 star rating: ***When God Broke Grandma's Heart***: WHEN LIFE GETS YOU DOWN, PICK THIS BOOK UP, it wrapped its arms around me. A wonderful read. Congratulations on an inspiring work.

<u>A reviewer, a reader in Kentucky:</u> Internet 5 star rating: ***When God Broke Grandma's Heart***: Well written, heartwarming, overcoming heartbreak through God, touches your heart. A worthwhile read for all generations.

<u>A reader:</u> Internet 5 star rating: ***When God Broke Grandma's Heart:*** a must read for all generations. FANTASTIC!

<u>A reviewer</u> Internet 5 star rating: ***When God Took Grandma Home***: Moves you, captivating.

<u>A reviewer, a Kentucky reader:</u> Internet 5 star rating: ***When God Took Grandma Home***: MUST READ! Touching story of life's tragedies and how lessons learned from these heartbreaking events can turn into blessings.

Novel Characters

Grandma: Grandma's life was filled with sibling betrayal and marital abuse. Her love of God, home remedies and famous boxing stance touches the heart.

Sarah: Sarah helps Grandma write her journal, learns about God's plan of salvation and the enemy who wants to harm her. She carries on Grandma's legacy of faith.

Matt: Matt, Sarah's husband, has a rock-like faith but when he loses a loved one, struggles with his anger with God, until he has a miraculous experience of faith.

Paul: Paul is Matt's older brother who earned a Captain's license for a seagoing tugboat. His faith sustains him despite enduring terrible circumstances.

Mary and Kevin: Mary and Kevin become Matt and Sarah's neighbors and friends. Mary's panic attacks end when God brings a miracle they never thought possible.

Elizabeth: Elizabeth adopts Rebecca, loses her husband twelve years later, is confronted with a potentially deadly illness and searches for Rebecca's birth mother.

Rebecca: Rebecca is Elizabeth daughter and Jayden's friend. Her father's death, the illness her mother faces, and a series of challenges at college almost destroy her.

John: John, a deacon, lost his wife to a debilitating disease, becomes Elizabeth's friend, and helps his daughter and grandson through a difficult divorce.

Jayden: Jayden is John's grandson and becomes Rebecca's friend. He has learned that prayer helps solve problems and he and Rebecca begin to share their faith.

Wade and Ruth: Wade is Jim's boss and friend who adopts two children from Iraq. Ruth is Jayden's mother and John's daughter who struggles to let go of the past.

Joshua and Debbie: Joshua, Sarah's younger brother, was demanding and judgmental until Caleb stepped in. Debbie looks to Joshua's family to be her role models.

Caleb and Ann: Caleb is Sarah and Josh's older brother and the family looks to him as they once looked to Grandma. Ann, Caleb's wife harbors a secret sadness.

Barbara and Jim: Barbara, Matt's sister is also Sarah's close friend. Her husband Jim plays devil's advocate in family debates, and matchmaker for his friend Wade.

Heza and Bara: Heza and Bara endured a suicide bomber attack when Bara was one and one half years old and Heza as she was born. They are adopted by Wade.

Chaldeth: Chaldeth is a fallen angel sent to destroy Grandma's family. He plots to bring great heartache to Rebecca and Jayden and their family to break their faith.

Durk: Durk, abused by a cruel father, is a sophomore at the college Rebecca and Jayden attend. He brings great harm to Rebecca and Jayden but Jim gives him a second chance and Jayden and Rebecca offer him forgiveness.

Professsor T. Nagorra, and Emils, and Dean Peerca: These tenured professors befriend Durk and engage in activities which bring harm to the students and the campus.

Professors Doog and Sendnik, and President Legna: These three share a faith in God, a love for their country, and desire to be role models. They help save the campus.

General Information

To become a distributor
To purchase books for a fund-raiser
To arrange a speaking engagement
To contact the author
To provide a review of Helen's books

email the author at:
helen@helenglowacki.com

Books, book descriptions, Domestic and International shipping rates, credit card purchases via Pay pal, and many of Helen's Facebook articles are available at the author's website at:
www.helenglowacki.com

Copies of Helen's books are available in the United States and Internationally through Helen's website and through most Internet booksellers.

They are also available in the UK through Matthew Burniston Distributors: phone 0776 0218 048, and in Pretoria, South Africa through Ambrose Damon: phone 072 380 8329, or Colette van Loggerenberg via Berg Distributors in Pietermaritzburg, South Africa: phone 082 748 5697.

Website by Daniel Landolfi

www.ingramcontent.com/pod-product-compliance
Lightning Source LLC
LaVergne TN
LVHW100140061126
851857LV00010B/174
9781450790758